THE KID FROM DEL RIO

- An Autobiography -

Ruben Michael Lara

To Tom & Rose Durst

Ruben (Rudy) Lara

My Parents
Adolfo Hernandez Lara
Julia Mendez Lara

DEDICATION

To the memory of my parents, Adolfo Hernandez Lara and Julia Mendez Lara to whom I owe a beautiful upbringing.

To my son, Robert Michael Lara and my daughter, Ruby Michelle Moore, both of whom I am very proud.
I dedicate this book especially to my grandchildren, Jessica Lara Moore, Jake and Joshua Lara, each having enriched an already wonderful life.

ISBN 13: 978-0-9816591-0-7
First Printing 2008

Maple Press Inc.
Telephone: 408-297-1000
E-mail:print@maplepress.net

MAPLE PRESS

Published by Cactus Rose Publishing
6138 Oneida Drive
San Jose, California 95123
Library of Congress Control Number 2008902696

For orders and all other general information contact:
Cactus Rose Publishing at:
Telephone: 408-972-5559
E-mail: cactusrose56@wmconnect.com

ACKNOWLEDGEMENTS

The family photographs in this book, for which I am very grateful, are from various family members who, fortunately for me, have preserved such memorable history.

Pictures of Del Rio are from the archives of Warren Studios in Del Rio as shown in Douglas Braudaway's book: Del Rio – Queen City of The Rio Grande. Also, pictures of my favorite swimming hole, the nostalgic Moore State Park, were generously provided by Greg Eckhardt's web site: mail@ewardsaquifer.net.

I thank the Whitehead Memorial Museum and the Val Verde County Historical Commission, whose publication, La Hacienda, shed a treasure of information on the history of my hometown and also for its publication, A History of Del Rio as compiled by A.E. Gutierrez, this narrowing the history of Del Rio down to my community of San Felipe.

The Desk Top Publishing Staff at Silicon Valley College, whose efforts I appreciate and to Rodney Cortez of Western Career College who gave me a helping hand.

Most sincerely, an indebtedness to my grandaunt, Eloisa Hernandez Lara, whose own hand-written, biographical manuscript shed an insight to my genealogy; information of which, otherwise, I would not have known.

CONTENTS

The Winter of My Life
By
Ruben Michael Lara

In the warmth and comfort of my living room
I find myself looking out my window
at the encroachment of an early autumn
upon a summer's ending

The leaves of brilliant yellows and burnt sienna
begin the cycle of their destiny
as they spiral downward, hesitantly,
in an undulating dance, thus prolonging
their final cycle

I am compelled to go out and meet this ritual
and as I walk along the sidewalk,
I feel upon my face, the cooling warmth of autumn
upon my back, I feel the warmth of summer cooling

The leaves fall to the ground in panic
in an attempt to flee, in scattered fear,
knowing full well the destiny that awaits them
as I know mine is near

CHAPTER 1

THE FOUNDING OF DEL RIO

Every small town has its own history; every small town has those personal elements of its founding, the cause and the story of its settlement. Every small town also has its own landmarks, those nostalgic elements that were part of our childhood, and the very same elements that nostalgically, still bind us now.

Del Rio, Texas, like any of these small towns, has its own colorful history; and as in James Mitchner's novel, *Centennial*, Del Rio has its very own ancestral landmarks, those familiar landmarks with which generations of Del Rioans grew up, and which are the nostalgic bond that keeps our childhood alive.

In describing the surrounding land around which the town of *Centennial* was to develop, Mr. Mitchner devoted an entire chapter of the very earliest times of this area. His description is vivid, compelling, and acutely detailed. It establishes some very definitive landmarks that early man witnessed and which played an on-going part in the history of that fictitious town.

The founding of Del Rio is a microcosm of the fictional *Centennial*; surely, the same can be said of any small town. The landmarks that preceded the founding of Del Rio, and which have been of great respect and nostalgia throughout the generations, are the San Felipe Springs and Round Mountain, or better known to us Del Rioans as *La Loma De La Cruz*, which literally translated, means, *The Hill of the Cross*. This endearing name for this particular landmark will be explained later in this chapter. Then of course, there's the Rio Grande, of which Del Rio is the Queen City.

The San Felipe Springs have been the lifeline of Del Rio since this small southwest town was founded. In fact, these springs played a most significant role in the founding of Del Rio. The San Felipe Creek, formed by three of these springs, is remembered by those of my generation with nostalgic fondness; it gave us excellent fishing, and it was in this creek that we learned to swim. Horseshoe Park, on the northern part of the creek, has always been a community-gathering place, especially at Easter time. The most popular swimming hole in Del Rio happens to be at this park. Gregg Eckhardt's website *edwardsaquifer.net/ sanfelip.html*, provided me with the following information: The San Felipe Springs are the fourth largest in Texas, with larger springs being in New Braunfels and San Marcos, both cities being along Highway 35 and within fifty miles north of San Antonio. Just on the outskirts of Del Rio, extending over one mile north of Highway 90, are the ten springs that feed San Felipe Creek. Prior to researching Mr. Eckhardt's website, I had always been under the impression that there was only one spring, the one that is a short distance from highway 90. There are three other springs in the vicinity of the only one I was aware of, the others being along one mile north from this spot. The source spring is about half mile north of Highway 90, a narrow, graveling road off the highway, leading to it.

The springs and the San Felipe Creek have quite a history dating back to 1590. It is believed that a European by the name of Gaspar Castano de Sosa, may have been the first foreigner to see this area. This beautiful, life-giving landmark was there during the Spanish Missionaries' march across the vastness of the southwest. Following the Spanish conquest of the Aztecs in Mexico and after the establishment of missions throughout

2

the southwest that included California and the Oregon region, a mission was established in the vicinity of the San Felipe Springs. The name San Felipe Del Rio, (Saint Phillip of the River), is thought to have been given by these early Spanish Missionaries upon their arrival at this location in 1635, on St. Phillip's Day. To us kids, in the forties, all along its length, the San Felipe Creek provided many Tom Sawyer/Huckleberry Finn adventures. In his website, Mr. Eckhardt notes Captain S.G. French's description of the San Felipe Creek in 1849:

> *To the north of the road, and half mile distant, there is a beautiful spring of water, fifty feet in diameter at the surface, the sides of which incline towards a center, like an inverted cone, and then, sinking to a cylindrical form to a depth of twenty-eight feet through a soil of hard clay, afford a passage for the water to rise. The water comes to the surface with a slight ebullition, and flows off in a volume that would fill a cylinder two feet in diameter. This spring is the source of the San Felipe; as it flows on, the volume of its water is increased by other large springs, on either side; until it becomes a creek, when it empties into the Rio Grande, eight miles below the crossing, some thirty feet wide and several feet deep. Near its junction with the Rio Grande, its banks are shaded with large groves of pecan, maple, elm, and mulberry trees*

One legend has it that, sometime around 1862, a rancher by the name of James Taylor from nearby Rio Grande City had some horses stolen by a small band of Kickapoo Indians. He quickly sent some of his ranch hands to retrieve the horses but the horse thieves had too much of a head start and probably made their way across the Rio Grande into Mexico by way of what is now Del Rio. Although the ranch hands didn't come back with the horses, they didn't come back empty-handed; they reported to Mr. Taylor that they had come upon some amazing springs while in pursuit of the Kickapoo. With great excitement, they went on to describe the ranching and agricultural possibilities offered by the springs. Mr. Taylor, along with his wife, Doña Paula Losoya, moved to the area of the springs in the early 1860's and very soon thereafter petitioned the government for a land grant around the San Felipe Springs. The grant being issued, the Taylors moved their ranching business around 1862 to what is now Moody property, not far from where the San Felipe Creek empties into the Rio Grande.

The real beginnings of Del Rio proper began in the late 1800's with the direct efforts of Mr. James Taylor and his wife, Dona Paula Losoya. Mr. Taylor became very involved with the development of the irrigation system, being a member of the San Felipe Agricultural, Manufacturing and Irrigation Company in 1869. Soon, the San Felipe Creek was dammed near the springs; tributary canals were built, thus bringing much needed water to the surrounding area. Not long after their arrival, Mr. Taylor passed away and Dona Paula Losoya, along with her sister, Doña Refugio Losoya, proceeded to have a large hacienda built, the labor coming from local Mexicans who at the time, lived in a community of underground shelters called "Las Sapas", these being simple, mud-roof, underground shelters covered with tree branches and brush for the roofs. The headquarters of the hacienda still stands in Del Rio; this is the original Losoya house located on the corner of East Nicholson and Hudson Drive, where a historical marker now stands.

The Losoya sisters became very rich, and with many labor hands living in the Hacienda, and the abundance of water fed by the irrigation canals, sugarcane was planted. Growth in the San Felipe community continued with the construction of a sugarcane mill and a flourmill. Additionally, an ice plant was built alongside the creek that produced electricity, as well as the ice. The hacienda became the home for many of the Las Sapas families and eventually many of these people started moving into the vicinity of the San Felipe Creek, where they wound up making their own homes. During the late 1860's, the hacienda was the political, religious and economical center of the community, which eventually was named San Felipe Del Rio. In 1876, however, the name was shortened to Del Rio because another city was found to have the name, San Felipe Del Rio. Thus, the town of Del Rio was born, this little town where my childhood was to take place in that community still known today as San Felipe.

From the Del Rio Chamber of Commerce website, and from Douglas Braudaway's *Del Rio –Queen of The Rio Grande*, I extracted the following information: Val Verde County, of which Del Rio is the County seat, has a lot of pre-historic records in the form of pictographs found in various caves. Some of these date 4,000 years B.C. The closest to Del Rio and most prolific in pictographs is Seminole Canyon near present-day Lake Amistad, twelve miles west of Del Rio. Other sites show evidence of Indian life in this area as long as 10,000 years ago. I wonder if Round Mountain was around at this time. All of this colorful history was all around me during my childhood, but only recently have I become aware of it, and I am very glad I did get to visit Seminole Canyon on one of my periodic trips to Del Rio.

Another bit of colorful history is the town of Langtry, a tourist attraction not far from Del Rio. In 1885, local citizen Roy Bean was elected Justice of the Peace. The legendary Judge Roy Bean became to be known as the enforcer of "Law West of the Pecos." Books, movies and a television series, were based on the colorful life of Judge Roy Bean. At some point during his tenure as Judge of the territory, the Judge became enamored with an English actress by the name of Lily Langtry, so he named the town Langtry and furthermore, named his bar-court-saloon "The Jersey Lily." Whoever painted the sign, misspelled "Lily" and to this day, the sign reads: "The Jersey Lilly." The actor, Paul Newman, played the part of Judge Roy Bean in the movie "The Life and Times of Judge Roy Bean" in 1972. Both Judge Roy Bean and his son, Sam, are buried at the Whitehead Museum grounds in Del Rio.

Round Mountain, or "La Loma De La Cruz" as we knew it, is actually a small hill located on the far, southeast edge of the city limits and quite close to School No. 2, one of the grade schools I attended. This small hill was called La Loma De La Cruz, because in the late 1800's, the Losoya Hacienda was occasionally attacked by small bands of hostile Indians and it is believed that Doña Paula Losoya had those killed in such skirmishes, buried on this hill and had the cross placed there. Another thought is that it was a religious gesture, with the cross overlooking the community. There is another legend concerning this hill, and that is, that the Losoya sisters had amassed such a huge fortune, they had it buried on this legendary hill. To us kids, this hill held an ominous cloud over it. In addition, the hill was overlooking the cemetery, and all of this was scary to us. In recent years, I've approached the base of this hill; it now looks so small, with the surrounding landscape pretty much as it was when I was kid; a kid too scared too go near there after sunset.

This history, the founding of Del Rio, I've learned of recently; the Del Rio I remember is in the pages of this story, a story of my childhood, a story of a way of life that is long gone...it was a good way.

Through my childhood, this is the house I always called home. It is shown here on one of the lots my father left us. Originally, the house was located at 610 Esquivel Street, which is less than one mile southwest from this property.

As shown, the house is filled with antiques my sister Minnie collected through several years. At the time I took this photograph, Minnie lived directly across the street.

The old ice plant...photo taken in 1888
(Photo courtesy of the Whitehead Memorial Museum and
the Val Verde County Historical Commission Publication:
La Hacienda)

This photo shows my paternal great-grandparents.
L. to R.: granduncle Felix, granduncle David (baby). great-
grandmother Florencia Balboa Hernandez, Lucrecia (unknown to me), my great-grandfather, Nazario Hernandez.
On the far right is granduncle Juan. On this day, my great-
grandmother and her children took great-grandfather his
lunch and spent the hour with him.

CHAPTER 2

INSIDE DEL RIO

Del Rio is a small, southwest border town that through my childhood was and still is, one of those small American towns where "everybody knows everybody." It permeates a relaxed, easy-going way of life; it's a great place for the retiree.

Interstate 10, from El Paso, Texas, goes southeast to Van Horn where Highway 90 intersects it north to south. At this junction, and continuing southeast, Highway 90 passes through Marfa, where the popular movie *Giant*, was filmed. From Marfa, Highway 90 continues on through Alpine, Marathon, Sanderson and Dryden, each with their own little history. It is approximately 300 miles from Van Horn to Del Rio.

In Del Rio, Highway 90 cuts through the west part of town, this section of the highway 90 having been named Veterans Blvd. in recent years. Upon reaching Gibbs, Highway 90 makes a left-hand turn and continues, almost due east, towards San Antonio, approximately 150 miles away. Between Del Rio and San Antonio, one passes through the colorful, small towns of Brackettville, Uvalde and Hondo, where a few miles west of these towns, begins a beautiful section of Texas known as *Hill Country*.

In the opposite direction from the intersection of Gibbs and Highway 90, and four blocks distant, is S. Main Street. Turning south at this intersection and six blocks distant, Main

9

is intersected first by Losoya, then by Greenwood, and then by Canal St. Between Losoya and Canal St., on Main Street, lies the downtown I remember, the downtown of my childhood. This is where all those nostalgic stores were, the principal ones being Walgreens, Kress, Sears and Roebuck, Montgomery Ward, Ross Drugstore, the Guarantee and a Piggly-Wiggly store. The Texas Theater and the Rita Theater were between Greenwood and Canal, across from each other and half a block apart. The Rita is now Paul Poag Theater where live shows and other social events are held. The only thing left of the Texas Theater, is the building that housed it, and the name: "TEXAS" barely legible on the north wall.

The intersection of Greenwood and S. Main Street is of great nostalgia to me, as Greenwood was the route we most often took into town from my house on Esquivel Street. Turning left on Main from Greenwood took us through that *Norman Rockwell* section of downtown. The Texas Theater was where I went to see most of the early forties western heroes such as Gene Autry, Roy Rogers, Tim Holt, Tex Ritter, The Durango Kid, Red Ryder and several other legendary cowboys. One western hero that I do not remember having seen then, is John Wayne, who used to play in B movies as a singing cowboy; in *The Three Musketeers* movies, he was the lead member. As it turned out, it is John Wayne who is my all-time, cowboy hero, and next to Abe Lincoln, the epitome of American backbone.

In addition to the westerns, we were thrilled by the Tarzan movies, the super heroes, Superman, Captain America and Captain Marvel. I also remember a serial on another superhero, The Phantom. Other genres included *Wolfman, Frankenstein,* and the *Bowery Boys.* Along with two movies, we got to see cartoons, *Movietone News*, and a serial that kept you coming back to see the hero get out of the impossible mess he had gotten himself into the week before, all of this for nine cents, which by the way, were hard to get.

I went to the Rita Theater often, but not as often as I did to the Texas. Both of these dear theaters hold major, nostalgic memories that are deeply stored in the minds of all of us old "kids" who lived through the forties era.

There's a Gene Autry movie that I went to see at the Texas with my older brother Dofo, and one of our next-door neighbors. In one segment of the movie, a gang of bad guys is chasing Gene. Gene comes to a cliff where the only escape for him and his horse, Champ, is to jump over the cliff and into the river below. Gene and Champ come out on the other side of the river and as they ride away, we see that Gene not only still has his hat on, but he is also completely dry.

On the way home, we usually passed by the legendary bridge, "El Puente Del Martillo" or in English, the Bridge of The Hammer, thusly referred to because someone, supposedly was bludgeoned to death with a hammer at this place. Just before the bridge, there is a narrow irrigation canal that is a tributary formed by a dam across the San Felipe Creek. My brother, four years older than I, and his friend, two years older than my brother, decided to jump across the canal. With both of them easily having jumped across, they stood watching as I prepped myself to jump across. Finally, getting enough courage, I jumped as far as I could, only to land on the tips of my feet, at which point, gravity took over and I fell into the canal. For many, many, many years after that incident, my brother would tell friends and relatives that I had jumped into the canal just to see if I would come out dry on the other side, just as Gene and Champ had.

North of Greenwood, towards Losoya, Main Street continues northwest for some distance. On this side of downtown, there were other businesses, including the Princess Theater, but I seldom went in that direction; that is, I don't have much recollection of that side of downtown, in fact, the only exception I do recall, is the few times I did go to the Princess theatre.

I've always thought of the Texas theater as being at the end of S. Main, but actually, S. Main continues for several blocks beyond Canal, an area with which, to this day, I am not very familiar. What I do remember, is that just past the Texas Theater, we would cross S. Main and turn left at the corner onto Canal Street, aptly named, as it parallels the San Felipe Creek for two blocks. Canal then makes a gradual southeast turn, crosses the creek over Canal Bridge, goes southeast for three blocks, and comes to a tee with Guillen. This junction is the southeast corner of a square block on which Brown Plaza was built. The other streets making up the square block are Cantu, which crosses Guillen at the northeast corner, where it tees with Cisnero Street, this completing the square.

Brown Plazas, or *La Plaza*, as we called it, was the gathering place where many holiday events took place, notably the Fourth of July, and Cinco de Mayo. The Plaza was comprised of businesses that included more than a few bars, pool halls and other, more family-oriented businesses. Of notable remembrance are two businesses, each a landmark in its own right, being remembered by the name of the proprietors as much as by the name of the business. One of these was a photography salon known as Treviño's; the other, a tailor shop, was known as Guzman's, both of these two businesses being as much of a fixture in the community as was the San Felipe Creek itself.

The land for La Plaza was donated by Mr. G.W. Brown in 1908, the same year the very first school I went to, School Number1, was built. This school has always been known as *La Escuela Amarilla*, (The Yellow School), this name coming by way of the light brown, yellowish brick used for the building. School Number1 replaced the original school built in 1883. This was a wood-frame school that had been built on the same property where School Number 1 now stands, except that the old school was on the west side of the property, facing Front Street, whereas, School Number1 faced Chapoy Street, both streets on corners with Cantu, and just two blocks southeast from La Plaza.

On my way to School Number1, I usually took Esquivel four blocks down to Taini, turning east, two blocks onto Chapoy, and then five blocks south, to the corner of Chapoy and Cantu, where the school was. There were a few other routes I could take, and each, eventually would lead to Chapoy. Two blocks east of Chapoy Street is Garza Street, which goes northeast towards the community of my childhood, *el barrio de San Felipe*, that part of Del Rio that I called home. Along Garza Street, between McMlymont on the southern side, and Waters Ave. on the northern side, is my old Alma Mater, San Felipe High School, home of the *Mustangs*. It is no longer a high school, and it is now called San Felipe Middle School; it will always be San Felipe High to me. I lived on Waters Ave. for one year, while I was in the fourth grade. The little house I lived at was directly across from the football stadium. The last time I drove by the stadium, it looked like an empty lot, sadly unkempt.

It was while living on Waters Ave. that I had a severe appendicitis attack, which I will discuss in a later chapter. Also, while living here, I used to catch tarantulas in the backyard; most of the backyard was bare, hard dirt and I would watch the tarantulas crawl into their holes. I caught the tarantulas by running the water hose in the hole for a short time, and eventually, the hairy front legs of the large spider would crawl out, right into a waiting jar I was holding. I kept these tarantulas for a while and then let them go. Now, whenever I see these creatures at some pet shop, the Waters Ave. backyard comes to mind, and so does the memory of the appendicitis attack.

Del Rio has always been a small town. The estimated population in 2006 was under forty thousand and during the late forties, it didn't even reach twenty thousand. At any rate, Del Rio is the county seat of Val Verde County with the surrounding terrain being mostly rolling hills with a variety of vegetation that gives it an "oasis" connotation in contrast to the open, dry rangeland west of the city limits. In the area along the Rio Grande, the grounds are very fertile and dotted with green valleys, this, making the area choice land, where most of the farming and agriculture took place. Crops grown on this section

13

of Del Rio included sugarcane, peaches, pears and an assortment of vegetables; pecan trees and mulberry trees were common throughout Del Rio. The development of Del Rio started in this area as a result of the San Felipe Creek and the ensuing irrigation canals. This is the area where a settlement took root, but it was to be west of the San Felipe Creek that most of the real development has taken place; east of the creek has shown very little development since the forties; it's still pretty much as I remember it.

San Felipe Creek was, and still is, along with Laughlin Air Force Base, the lifeline of Del Rio. It was also the dividing and distinct line between east and west; a distinction clearly seen in the paved streets and sidewalks on the west side versus the unpaved streets and bare yards on the east side; such was the barrio of San Felipe, mi barrio. The contrast is still visible, although the east side has shown some improvement. I always remember that west of the creek, the yards had green, well-manicured lawns, along with the surrounding, complimenting landscape. Pecan trees and loquat trees could be seen on many yards; additionally, these homes had sidewalks and indoor plumbing. At night, we kids used to sneak onto some of these yards and take some loquats or pecans. Now, whenever I see a fruit tree on somebody's yard, I knock on the door and ask if I can "steal" some. I explain that this satisfies the nostalgia of my childhood; they always comply.

In a way, I am glad to see that the community in which I spent my childhood hasn't changed much; I can see many places the way I remember them. Unfortunately, as a grownup, I take the lack of change in the San Felipe community as a slap in the face to the pride and the history of that colorful community.

Photo of South Main Street. The Texas Theater is in the foreground; Kress Store can be seen in the background. Main Street was not a one-way street during my childhood. (Photo courtesy of Douglas Braudaway's book, *Del Rio - Queen City of The Rio Grande*

La Loma De La Cruz (Round Mountain, or literally
translated, "The Hill of The Cross").

La Plaza - The community center for annual celebra-
tions, particularly, Cinco De Mayo and Fourth of
July.
I believe the auto shown is coming from the direction
of La Escuela Amarilla (School Number 1) on Cantu.
The school is on the corner of Cantu and Chapoy.

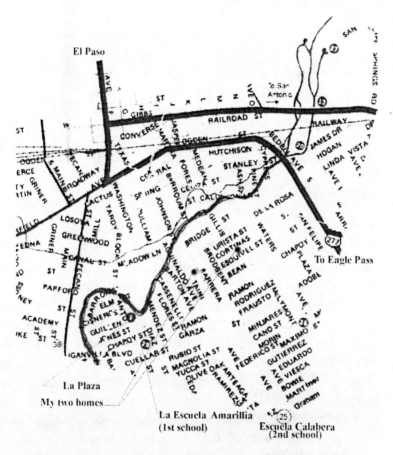

El Paso

La Plaza
My two homes

La Escuela Amarillia
(1st school)

Escuela Calabera
(2nd school)

To Eagle Pass

At lower left, on the corner of Cantu and Chapoy is the first school I attended, School Number 1, better known as La Escuela Amarilla, (The Yellow School) due to the brick construction of the building. At lower right is the second school I attended, School Number 2, better known as La Escuela Calavera, (The Skull School) due to its proximity to the cemetery.

CHAPTER 3

THE SAN FELIPE CREEK

During my childhood, and up to present times, I was not aware that the San Felipe Springs were comprised of ten springs. As mentioned earlier, only during recent research from Gregg Edwards website, *www.edwardsaquifer.net/sanfelip.html*, have I found this out. Further, from this website, I have learned that three of the springs are in such close proximity to the one spring I was aware of. Two springs flow directly into the San Felipe Creek; two others flow into what is called Blue Lake, from which one branch of the water flow, merges with the creek just south of the park area. This park, too, I have always known as State Park (actually named Moore Park) only to find out now, that it is called Horseshoe Park. I don't care what it's called; part of my heart lingers there. I was also not aware of Blue Lake as such; we used to call this pocket of water, *blue waters,* and we generally stayed away from it because it was too deep for most of us kids. Some of the older boys, including my brother, Dofo, used to dive off the railroad bridge into this deep water.

The boys that used to dive off of the bridge were all very good swimmers, and among them was an eight, or nine year old kid that was as good a swimmer as the older boys, and better than some. He was such a good swimmer, that his nickname was *La Porcha*, or perch.

One day, I stood along the bank and watched with other kids as these older daredevils took turns diving off the bridge. The trick was to dive and not come up until the diver grabbed a handful of "sea weeds" to prove that he had reached bottom. When my brother's turn came up, I remember holding my breath as soon he hit the water. I felt that by the time I ran out of breath, he would be coming up. When I couldn't hold my breath any longer, I took another deep breath and held it in again, thinking that he would surely come up by then; but he didn't. Finally, as I was about to take another deep breath, this one with great concern, my brother popped up out of the water, waving the vegetation he had pulled from the bottom. The eight-year-old boy, "La Porcha", was one of the participants, and he too, was successful.

Most of the time was spent at the favorite swimming hole a few yards from Blue Lake and just past the Highway 90 overpass. A short distance, and directly south from this overpass, is that spring which I have always known to be the source of the creek. I visit this spot every time I go to Del Rio; I read the Historical marker and then walk around the building that houses the water works and watch the water flow into what is the beginning of San Felipe Creek. Behind the small building, the water emerges into what looks like a swimming pool. From here, the water cascades into the narrow portion and makes its way south, all the way to the Rio Grande. Here, I stare at this narrow stream as it cascades into what is the beginning of the San Felipe Creek. Not far from the spring's source, one can follow the narrow creek up to the underpass of Highway 90. At this point, the creek is deeper and one can actually jump in and swim under the overpass and come up into that beautiful, old friend, that nostalgic swimming hole.

In the vicinity of the source spring, I used to walk along the creek, retrieving errant golf balls, these, for five cents each from thankful golfers. The County Club is adjacent to the creek and borders that area where the spring still produces an average of 30,000,000 gallons of pure water every day. The Historical

19

marker still shows the amount to be 90,000,000 gallons, which the springs did produce, at one time. I have a whopper of a fish story that took place between the spring source and Highway 90 overpass; the fish story is true and is covered in another chapter.

Another favorite spot that I was very aware of, and is not far from Moore Park, was the "Pig Pen," so called because it was one of only two animal-drawn, vehicle crossings during the early years of the San Felipe community. The Pig Pen was a shallow part of the creek where supposedly, farmers would cross their stock to market. This is actually the spot where many of us kids learned to swim as it was shallow enough not to fear, yet deep enough to swim in. In my childhood, I remember car owners driving into this spot where they would wash their cars, and then continue across. This spot is very different now; an eyesore overpass adjacent to it, marring the old crossing.

At any given spot along the San Felipe Creek, kids would have a rope hanging off a tree branch that extended over the water's edge. This was our "Tarzan" swing which we would ride as far as it would go, and then jump off, right at its apex. It was also common to tie a discarded automobile tire, which we would ride just like a swing, and eventually, jump off. Some trees along the banks of the creek had "vines" long enough to swing from. We would climb up the tree and make our way to the branch from which the vine hung and we'd swing on it, just like we did from the ropes. I tell you, the San Felipe Springs, the creek that these springs spewed, and all the beautiful spots along its banks; all of these are a major part of my childhood, firmly and nostalgically imbedded within the confines of this old man's mind.

Grapevines, cattails, pecan trees, mulberry trees and hackberry trees surround the San Felipe Springs. This type of vegetation was typical, but as mentioned, of more abundance along the southern end of the creek bordering the Rio Grande. Along its banks, the creek also had a good share of bamboo outcroppings, which offered us a nice fishing rods as well as the material with which we made our kites.

From the Highway 90 overpass, the San Felipe Creek provides many beautiful scenic spots with its crystal-clear water and lush landscape along its bank. Its length, beginning just above Moore Park, snakes southeast, cutting through the eastern section of town where it makes a horseshoe turn upward a few blocks above Brown Plaza where it crosses Canal Street, almost at the peak of the horseshoe. The horseshoe curve of the creek continues southward and then circles back and goes straight for three blocks, as if heading back to its source. After another turn, once again heading southeast, the creek makes one last turn and heads directly south, where it begins a meandering course that eventually turns southwest, where it completes its journey, emptying into the Rio Grande. I could probably write a nice little book on just the San Felipe Creek, as it has such a colorful history, but of greater importance to me, is that it is a very poignant and profound part of my childhood; during the forties, the San Felipe Creek was the center our childhood in Del Rio.

Horseshoe swimming hole, just past the horseshoe bridge shown below. (Photo from Greg Eckhardt's website: edwardsaquifer.net/sanfelip.html.

Horseshoe swimming hole. This is the spot we used the most. Just a few yards behind, is Highway 90 and about a mile across the highway are the San Felipe Springs (see map).

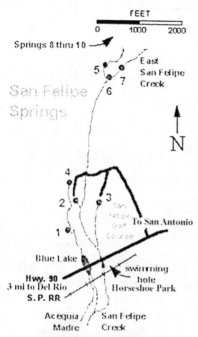

FEET

0   1000   2000

Springs 8 thru 10

5
7   East
San Felipe
Creek

6

San Felipe
Springs

N

San Felipe Springs. Number 3 spring is the only one I knew of until recently. It is from this spot to Highway 90 that I had an unbelievable fishing day.

4

2   3

San
Felipe
Golf
Course   To San Antonio

1

Blue Lake

Hwy. 90
3 mi to Del Rio
S. P. RR

swimming
hole
Horseshoe Park

Acequia
Madre   San Felipe
Creek

La Presa (The Dam). This is where we tried to walk across as kids. Three blocks to the right is the house we lived in when I was born. About one block to the left is the infamous El Puente De El Martillo (The Hammer Bridge) so called because some-one, supposedly, was bludgeoned to death here, with a hammer.

23

CHAPTER 4

MY FATHER'S WORK

My father, Adolfo Hernandez Lara, worked as a ranch hand, principally, at sheep shearing, in several ranches in southwest Texas. These towns were not too far from Del Rio, but required that my father spend several weeks to several months at any one of these. Notably, he worked in Rocksprings, El Dorado, San Angelo and Johnson City.

Rocksprings, known for its wool and mohair production, provided a lot of work for my father; it was here that he met the queen, my mother, Julia Maldonado Mendez. Rocksprings has always been smaller than Del Rio, but interestingly enough, each has been recognized, respectively, as the mohair and the wool capitol of the world. There are still some relatives of my mother's living in Rocksprings, and I hope to visit them soon.

In my childhood, I enjoyed the visits to our relatives in Rocksprings. My cousins and I would invariably go out into the "wilderness," which was very similar in terrain as it was in Del Rio. Meanwhile, the adults would visit and prepare a barbecue for the evening. I was too young to think of such, but I wish I had been more aware of the Mendez family and asked about my grandparent's background; I have very little information on the Mendez family. One memory I have of one of our visits to Rocksprings is the time my father and an uncle butchered a pig. I was seven or eight at that time and I don't remember if it was a particular holiday, or just another family get-together. What I do remember is the pig that was being prepared for slaughter, was one tough pig. First of all, my father and an uncle had trouble catching the large pig. This alone, was very exciting for my cousins and me to watch. Once they subdued it, the poor pig refused to die. They shot it with what I would assume was a thirty caliber rifle and it took more than one shot. Finally, my father and my uncle carried out this unpleasant chore and prepared the pig for barbecuing. I wonder if this recollection is the reason why I prefer eating beef to pork meat.

On another occasion, I remember a goat being prepared for a festive family gathering. My cousins and I also found this experience exciting to watch. First, the goat's hind legs were tied and then it was lifted up and hung over a tree branch by its hind legs. The next part was too gruesome to watch, but we did; someone would cut the goat's throat and the blood would drain into a bucket. Goats were easier to kill, and I enjoyed the meat far better than pork. I do not remember if the blood was eaten, nor do I remember if it was used for any other purpose.

After the goat was butchered, it was barbecued in an open pit. The head was covered in a burlap sack and buried in a shallow hole, over which a fire was built. After several hours, the tasty meat was ready to eat. One bonus we kids got from barbecued goat head was that, when the meat was all eaten up, we would use the jawbones for pistols; they made excellent six-shooters for us poor kids. Also, there was a bone section, perhaps from the neck, that had a hole through it; this we used on our cowboykerchief, similar to what Hopalong Cassidy wore.

At another small ranching town where my father was working, I experienced a scary, yet beautiful memory; it was the first and only time I saw my father hit one of us, and it happened to be my brother, Dofo. At that time, I believe he was ten or eleven years old, so I must have been six or seven. It was my father's responsibility to take care of the ranch chores, which included tending a large flock of sheep, this, being the principal livestock on the ranch. On this particular afternoon, my brother, two brothers, (next-door neighbors of ours in Del Rio), and I, were putting the ranch sheepdog through its paces; that is, the older boys were. I was just a spectator, totally amused as the dog chased the sheep from one corral into another, and then out again. This "round up" was going on not too far from the small ranch house where we were living at the time. About an hour or so into our adventure, I heard my sister Locha calling out to my brother as she walked towards us. "Dofo!" "Father wants you!" Well, that ended our fun and it was also getting close to dinnertime, so we headed down towards the house.

My brother was ahead of the rest of us, with me following close behind. Ahead, I could see my father with his back to one of those fifty-gallon drums that was commonly used as an outdoor furnace. His hands were clasped behind him, as was customary, to keep warm. This time, that was not the case. As my brother approached, he barely got to ask my father, "Did you want to see me, dad?" Almost simultaneously, my father swung an arm around with a piece of rope in his right hand and struck my brother down. The blow didn't hit him squarely, as he was ducking and going down with the blow. I was shocked at what I was seeing! I turned tail and ran away from the house as fast as I could. There was a lot of open land, so I just took off, away from a very angry father.

As I was running and crying in fear, I could hear my father yelling angrily at my brother. Then I heard him calling me, and as I looked back, he was chasing after me! To this day, I can't believe that a grown ranch hand could not catch up to a little boy. As he chased me, my father made quick stops, picked up dirt clots and hurled them at me. Then, perhaps he was winded, because he stopped and yelled out, "Just wait when you get home!" Then he turned around and headed home. At that point, I had run out of room as I came up to a barbwire fence that was too high for me to climb over. In shear fear, I turned around looking at my father's back as he got farther and farther away. I slumped

26

down on the ground and cried my heart out. I was scared, and I had no idea what we had done wrong.

I sat there for what seemed like hours and soon, fear of darkness approaching won over my fear of a spanking. So with great trepidation, I wiped off the tears and headed home. My mother was coming towards me by this time, and as she guided me back home, she said, "Your father is taking a nap, go lie down by his side and I'll call you when dinner is ready." When I awoke, my father wasn't in bed and I was still scared. I timidly walked into the kitchen and joined the others for dinner. Nothing further was said of the incident, and I escaped my father's wrath. I didn't get spanked and that incident was the only time I ever saw my father discipline any one of us. He never yelled at us, and as I said, other than the above stated incident, he never spanked any one of us.

As to the incident that angered my father, it was my sweet angel mother that explained it to us, later. She told us that the sheep were getting close to having babies, and that what we were doing could have been very harmful to the flock and a big financial loss to the ranch owner. I didn't feel bad about what we had done because I didn't know we had done anything wrong, and I surely could not have understood the significance, then.

I remember the ranch owner as being a very kind, easy-going man. He used to spend time with me whenever he came by and watched me building forts or corrals with corncobs, which is a fond memory of mine. Corncobs were abundant, as this was one of the principal foods being fed to several pigs on the ranch, and I enjoyed building corrals or forts with the dried up corncobs; there were mounds of them on this ranch.

At this ranch, our living quarters were close to two corrals that were adjacent to each other. In one of the corrals was a beautiful prize stallion and in the other, a huge prize bull. One day, one of the two was acting skittish and this put the other on the defensive. The angry snorting of the bull and the equally angry neighing of the stallion quickly had us all running towards the corrals. The pounding of the hooves on the ground and the horse's powerful kicks at the fence were very frightening to me. The owner was summoned but by the time he got there, the two animals had broken through and were now in a horrible fight. Because of the veracity of the battle between these two beautiful and proud animals, we all watched helplessly, shocked at what we were witnessing. To this day, I wonder if the owner thought of putting either one of the two animals down while they fought, or whether he too, was just as frozen with shock. I also wonder which one he would have chosen to put down. Unfortunately, the end of the fight proved to be fatal to both animals, and what must have been very painful for the owner; both animals had to be put down.

. At an earlier time when these two magnificent animals lived side by side in their own corrals, my father told us that the owner had proudly mentioned to him that the animals had cost $10 thousand dollars each. As much as that amount of money was in those days, I know the owner would have paid much more than that to have them alive; it was a tragic loss. I'll always remember the ranch owner's a kindness and the heartbreak of having lost those two beautiful animals.

There was one unpleasant incident that occurred, perhaps in the same town, or perhaps during another season of my father's work, I really don't remember. In any case, the town that comes to mind is El Dorado, and I was six or seven. We had gone into town on a weekend to do some shopping and shortly, around noon, my father took us to a small restaurant for a hamburger. Even now, I can sense the distinct smell of the "on the grille" hamburgers and the onions as we approached the restaurant. At the door, my father stopped for a moment and then led us away to look for another place. I didn't understand why at the time, but later I was told by one of my older sisters that there was a sign on the door that read: "No Mexicans allowed."

For the first few years in California, my father worked in the fields right along with the family. In later years, he was in charge of the irrigation system for the fruit orchards and. I remember going with him, on occasion. The irrigation system began at a well that was housed in a shed that reminded me of the outhouses in Del Rio. From the piping coming out of this shed, my father would attach waterlines in both directions, left and right of the shed. These waterlines paralleled the front of the orchard and from these, my father attached the lines that went in-between the rows of trees; this watered the orchard, and the process would be repeated until all the rows had been watered.

One day, on a weekend, I experienced a clairvoyant incident involving the watershed. My father had gone to pick up his check and my mother and I were with him, most likely because we were going shopping in downtown San Jose and I was anxiously looking forward to going to the movies while they shopped.

My father drove to the orchard where he was currently irrigating and pulled up in front of the watershed. He got out of the car and went over to meet the man who was to give him the check, while my mother and I waited in the car. I could see my father and the man standing and talking by the side of the shed and then squatting down, looking out, towards the piping. They stood up again and walked along to the right of the watershed for a short distance, then stopped to check something else out. After a while, I was getting antsy, and as my father and the man started back towards the shed, I anxiously awaited their concluding their discussion.

They walked slowly back to the shed and then stopped to talk again! I felt very anxious at this point, and started hurrying them, mentally. My mother noticed my impatience and tried to console me. I just kept looking at the men as they stood up and headed back towards the watershed. Relieved, I started keeping time with their steps and as soon as they got to the watershed, I mentally continued tracing their imaginary steps while they were behind the shed; this, to make sure they weren't stopping again. At the very instant that my mind had them step out on the other side of the watershed, they in fact did. I didn't think much of that incident at the time, but I have experienced several other, similar incidents that bear mentioning; I have noted these in a later chapter.

Eventually, the latter years of my father's work was at Green Valley cannery in San Jose, from which he retired in the mid-sixties as nightshift supervisor. My father was a good man; throughout his life, he never shied away from work, and he always provided food and shelter, which, after all, are the very basic responsibilities of a man.

Grandfather Hilario Lara. My grandaunt, shown below, wrote in her memoirs that my great-grand mother was a Cherokee woman named Maria De Los Angeles Samaniego

Grandmother Faustina Hernandez Lomas. My grandparents were divorced and grandmother later married Francisco Lomas.

Granduncle Eugenio Lara and grandaunt Eloisa Hernandez Lara. He was my grandfather's brother and she was my grandmother's sister.

On a day off from the ranch. Father is on the right.

Father on another day off, maybe going courting a young lady from Rocksprings, Texas

The three Caballeros, three ranch hands going to town??? My father is seated.

Young lady on the right is mother with her two older sisters, my aunts Bernabe and Bonifacia

Mother as a teenager.

My mother - a young lady who was to rope the ranch hand from Del Rio

CHAPTER 5

A LITTLE BIT OF SALSA

In the forties and into the early fifties, racial prejudice against Mexican-Americans was an ongoing social illness. With the exception of a few relative minor incidents, I personally didn't experience any rejection based on this matter.

One of these "minor" incidents involved my brother Dofo and some of his friends. I was too young at the time and could not have understood its cause nor, certainly, its meaning. On this particular day, my brother had taken me with him to the San Felipe Creek, as he often did. I'm sure that taking me was not my brother's idea, but rather, a responsibility my mother placed on him, that is, to look after me. Usually, we went swimming or fishing, both of which were very common activities.

With us on this outing, were two of my brother's friends, with me following along, looking forward to swimming or just enjoying the creek' surroundings. Not long after we got to what was one of the favorite swimming spots, some yells came from across the creek. My brother and his friends responded in like kind and then all hell broke loose! A battle of rock throwing and slingshot-shooting broke out between several white kids on the other side of the creek and us. Neither side could really see the other because of the bamboo thicket and other tall shrubbery, including some large trees. One reason I remember that incident, is that my brother got hurt by a rock and was bleeding all the way home. This frightened me, although the injury wasn't serious and it was the only casualty of that foolish encounter.

Another, lighter incident, occurred when I was thirteen or fourteen. My best friend, Tony Treviño and I were going to the hospital to visit my girlfriend, Baby Calderon, whose nature of her illness I don't recall. As we walked along on the east side of Losoya Street towards the hospital, there came a yell from the other side of the street. Three older white teenage boys yelled at us, "Hey!" "You better speak English or we'll come over and beat you up!"

The only other such incident I remember, happened during a carnival on the west side of town. Again, my best friend Tony Treviño and I were walking back home and ahead of us, were four white girls. Tony and I were speaking Spanish, as we normally did. One of the girls turned around and told us that if we didn't stop talking behind their backs, they were going to call the police. Although we were just talking about the events while at the carnival, we understood their concern and spoke more quietly. Other than these incidents, during my childhood, and throughout my life, I never experienced racial discord and have always blended well with my multi-nationality friends.

CHAPTER 6

WEIRD HAPPENINGS

There was that incident where my father had gone to pick up his paycheck and I, anxious to get to the movies, "mentally" hurried him up. This was not the first "weird" incident I ever experienced. The very first one involved a hopscotch game at the time we lived on Esquivel Street. One day, in determining player order in a game of hopscotch, I experienced a "chance" occurrence. The players were my sister Locha, our next-door neighbor Alicia, and her brother, Chale. Turning our backs to a line some distance away, we each tossed a trinket, such as a coin, small-chain bracelet or some other small item, over our shoulders, towards the line; the one whose trinket landed closer to the line would be first, and so on. The dirt where we had drawn the line was very soft and loose. Alicia, who had tossed a very thin chain bracelet, lost it in the dirt. We all looked for it as carefully as we could around the general location, being careful not to bury it any deeper. After a while, we just couldn't find it! I thought to ask Alicia to stand at the same spot and toss a little pebble as best as she could remember having thrown the bracelet originally. She did, and amazingly, the pebble landed right on the spot, exposing the bracelet!

In later years, I was to do some things that are even more inexplicable to me. One of these happened while working at

FMC (Food Machinery Corporation). Coming back from lunch one day, I passed by some of my colleagues who had just finished playing cards. As I approached the one that was putting the cards away, I said, "cut the cards and I'll tell you what card comes up." Grinning, he shuffled the cards and asked me to call out the card. "Ace of spades," I said. Well, that is exactly the card that came up.

Other happenings, more surprising to me, concerning coins, occurred while working at Lockheed. In one case, I reached into my pocket and pulled out whatever coins I had. Showing the coins to a few of my co-workers, I told them that I would toss the coins and call out how many coins would be heads and how many would be tales. These things didn't work time after time, or at any given time anyone asked me to do it; it only happened when I had this "inner" feeling that I could do it, almost like a cocky confidence. I did this "coin tossing" successfully, several times.

Another variation involved tossing a mixture of coins and calling out the coins that would be heads and those that would be tails. I think I did this one a couple of times; each time I was successful, I didn't act surprised, but inside me, I was just as confounded as my colleagues.

CHAPTER 7

SCENT OF THE SEASONS

The seasons are very different today. True, the seasons here in California are typically different than the seasons in other states, including my home state of Texas. This, of course, is due to their respective geographical location. Just recently, on April 26, 2007, my friends Eddie Payne and Jorge Treviño (no relation to Tony) and I, went to the "Fiesta Days" in San Antonio, which was preceded with a two-day stop in Del Rio. One night, while Eddie and Jorge went to a casino in Eagle Pass, I was totally surprised that two tornadoes passed by. At the moment this was taking place, I was having dinner at Memo's with two friends of mine; one being my very first girlfriend, Baby Calderon and the other being Mario Barragan, who was my guide through this trip in Del Rio. Mario is also the person who led me to Douglas Braudaway's book, *Del Rio-Queen City of The Rio Grande.* My niece Elsa had tried to reach me on my cell phone to warn me about the impending tornados, but unknowingly, I had my cell phone set on silent and was not aware of the call. She called the restaurant and the phone was brought over to our table. Elsa went on to tell me that one tornado was heading our way, and that one was passing by, across the southern part of town.

As soon as we hung up, Baby left quickly to go home and check on her family, while Mario and I headed to his house to check on it. As we left the restaurant, a sudden downpour came down and thunder and lightening were all around us. In no time, the streets were flooded, and things got a little scary. Although the tornado did not hit, I had never been that close to one, and certainly, not in Del Rio! Later that night, a tornado did hit the next town of Eagle Pass, just fifty-five miles east.

The following morning, I read in the newspaper that Eagle Pass had incurred much damage, and in the bordering Mexican town of Piedras Negras, several lives were lost. Eddie and Jorge did not experience the wrath of the tornado. This experience was not, by any means, typical of the springs I remember in Del Rio. I suppose that the seasons I remember during my childhood, pose similar memories to those held by anyone of my generation in their respective towns. In Del Rio, I remember having a distinct spring, a distinct summer, a distinct fall and very definitely, a distinct winter. Each season brought us its own richness of life; each displayed its own individuality and beauty; this is how I remember the scent of seasons during my childhood.

Spring was a respite from the darkness and cold of winter, a respite from its thunderous lightening storms. Spring brought the freshness and the green of the land; it brought to us kids the outdoor activities, with Easter at Moore Park, leaving a special, nostalgic scent. Easter was one of those times when families in the community got together, a truly great celebration. The San Felipe Creek, through spring and into early autumn, offered many beautiful childhood adventures. I've met new friends from different parts of Del Rio with whom I did not share my childhood, but whose memories of the creek and of the forties, in general, pretty much parallel mine.

Summer meant school was out! It meant baseball on the streets, marble games, spinning tops, swimming and fishing; it meant hunting with our slingshots or our Red Ryder BB guns; summer meant eating watermelons and riding our Shwinn bicycles anywhere throughout the community. I remember the summers were hot, but I don't remember minding the heat then, as much as I do today. Those summer days were jubilant times, with the San Felipe Creek offering most of the fun. We kids learned to swim in this creek at a very early age. Fishing was a given, with the creek offering, not just an abundance of fish, but the fishing rods as well, from the bamboo patches along its banks. These banks also provided all the bait we needed in the form of large, earthworms.

Of the celebrations held at Brown Plaza, the Fourth of July made for a lot of excitement for us kids, from the blast of the powerful firecrackers the older boys popped, to the smaller ones we younger kids lit up and threw at each other's feet, not too smart, but fun and exciting. Then, there were the sparklers we waved high over our heads, running around in circles. In the streets of our neighborhood, it was common for us to put an empty food can on top of a firecracker with just the wick sticking out. We'd light it and run away as fast as we could. It was a thrill to see how high the can would go.

I think the newspaper was also located nearby the plaza. Many of us kids used to buy the paper here for five cents and go out and sell it for ten cents. This, and shoe shinning provided us with the money for the movies and usually, enough for a bag of popcorn and a soda. Sometimes we didn't have enough money for a soda and popcorn, so what many kids did, including yours truly, was to go to the back of the theater before the movie started, and gather up left-over popcorn from the not-quite-empty boxes from the previous showing; that's the way it was, back in the early forties!

Most of the summer was spent swimming, playing marbles, baseball or playing "kick the can", an exasperating form of "hide and seek." Hunting was another common pastime. Most of us had slingshots; a few of us were fortunate enough to have a Daisy Red Ryder BB gun. As with my very first bicycle, I didn't get my first BB gun until I was eleven. Today, I have three vintage Red Ryder BB guns, one each, on either side of my John Wayne posters on the entrance wall to my office, and the third one, above my desk, just under an Ivan Jesse Curtis large print titled, "All Of My Heroes Are Cowboys," which depicts twenty-two of the most popular cowboys of the forties.

One of the most memorable experiences during the summers was catching fireflies. Every night, they would put on quite a display of flashing lights and we would catch some of these and smear them on our tee shirts, or swipe them across our forehead so that we would "glow" for a few moments. I wonder if this is why they aren't seen anymore. I hope not; I miss that experience. Another thing we used to do with the fireflies was to catch a bunch of them and put them in a jar. In the darkness of the theatre, we'd turn them loose! It was great to see them flashing their twinkling light, now here, and then, in a blink, there; this was always a hit with the crowd.

The scent of autumn, I remember as a time of spiritual warmth, a time of giving; I remember the food basket drives we used have at school for Thanksgiving, filled with canned and dry goods, The food baskets we collected were then taken to selected needy families. Mind you, we were as poor as most of the families in our community of San Felipe, but unfortunately, there were some that were poorer.

A most poignant memory I have of this time is when I was selected to deliver two of the baskets. The son of the family selected was one of my classmates, and he was asked to go with me to show me the way to his house. We each carried a food basket, and as we walked in silence, I could see that his face was red and his eyes swollen with the tears he fought to hold back. His grandmother had passed away recently, and the pain of this loss, plus his pride and dignity of his family being one of the recipients of the food basket, must have weighed heavily on him. The silence was very awkward for both of us. I wonder, to this day if my eyes weren't a little swollen too; I felt so bad for him. Neither one of us spoke a word all the way to his house, nor on the way back to school; I will never forget that experience.

It was not yet too cold in early autumn and we were still able to play most of our outdoors games. The change in scenery around us was noticeable. Some trees made for a colorful fall;

their respective leaves turning a bright yellow, red-orange or burnt sienna with green leaves still mingling among this display of color. Autumn meant school was starting and by then I was actually looking forward to it. I especially looked forward to the Thanksgiving and Christmas activities, during which time we used to have school assembly programs, these, performed by the students! I was in the cast of a three-act play that was a non-holiday play. I played the part of a judge who had to deal with the vanities of the other characters in the cast. I remember handing out relief from their respective concerns, which in return, they gave up something else, such as their hearing or their eyesight. The third act had each individual begging the judge to bring him or her back as they were before; the jest of the play being that we should be satisfied with the way we are. I also remember that Tony and Baby were in the cast.

Autumn also brought the feel of the coming of school. This, too, I found somehow exhilarating. I still get that feeling every autumn; I miss school and I'm a big fan of the football season, which has always been huge in Texas. On my recent trip in Del Rio, and thanks to my niece, Elsa Jacobs, I was privileged with a personal visit to the San Felipe Exes Museum. I saw yearbook photos of my third and fourth grade "sweetheart", Nani. I had such a crush on this wonderful person for many years. To this day she remains as one of those people I hold in high esteem, and for whom I have the utmost respect and admiration. Photos of Nani in these early yearbooks and one photo of the 1948 football team brought a lump to my throat. Nani has always been such a pretty lady, and she was beautiful in these photos. The football photo was also heartfelt, in a different way, of course. At the top of the photo was the quarterback, Daniel Peña; at each side of the photo, in columns, were the rest of the team members. I could remember so many of the faces on that photo! It brought back a very powerful and proud moment; that team was one of the best teams San Felipe High ever had.

Now, winter, on the other hand, had its dark moments.

Seldom did we get snow in Del Rio during the winter months, although I do remember one year when we had enough snow to make a pretty good-size snowman. The dark sides of winter were the rain downpours, and the thunder and lightening storms that made me fear the earth was going to explode. But even in these dark, ominous nights, the family unity was intact and warm, as we all gathered around the radio and listened to the popular programs of the day; and of course, there were times when there was homework to be done!

Walking to school during the winter days was indeed, a chilly experience, but this too, was routine. Besides the fact that this was a way of life, what made it easy for us kids was that we all shared the experience walking as a group, and there was no room for sissies. I don't remember school busses being available throughout my school years in Del Rio; they certainly weren't in my neighborhood. In fact, few families had automobiles. Anyway, to us kids, walking to school was an adventure we shared, and our parents made sure we were well bundled up in warm clothing, including those silly caps with the long earflaps.

Some nights, I recall vividly, the rain being literally torrential, the lightening and that earth shattering thunder exploding around the house. This used to frighten me so much that I would hide under the covers. Except for my latest trip to Del Rio, I have never heard thunder as loud as those winter nights of my childhood. During these storms, it was routine to cover the windows and mirrors with sheets, a ritual that gave the storm an even more, ominous feel. Only now do I realize why this ritual was wise. Another routine at home during the rainy season, was the placing of pots and pans throughout the house in pursuit of the raindrops. There were always various leaky spots in the roof. Somehow, the drip, drip sound did not affect our sleep. I suppose it was actually soothing and actually helped our sleep, sort of like our very own, indoor waterfall. Only the blast of one of those powerful thunderous blasts would wake me up, and that's when the covers went over my head.

The highlight of the winters, of course, was Christmas. How

warm was our little house with the family gathered for dinner, and for us, the anticipation of what Santa Clause might bring. The gifts were meager, to say the least, but boy were they welcomed and appreciated. I remember how much my sister Locha and I enjoyed looking at all the Christmas toys in the Sears catalog. We would take turns choosing "left" or "right" pages, and whatever toys were on the respective pages, would be "ours." This was such an enjoyable fantasy. In reality, we typically, got an orange-red, mesh stocking filled with goodies. The "goodies" included bazooka bubble gum, an assortment of nuts, a banana or an orange…and a little toy. A toy for me would either be a whistle, a yoyo, a spinning top, or a small, simple wooden gun. How happy I was with these simple gifts.

Other nostalgic memories transcended the seasons; one of these is the music of the forties and early fifties! The big band dance music was the rage during those years. Tommy and Jimmy Dorsey were especially popular, but the band that is still considered the granddaddy of them all, was the Glenn Miller Orchestra. There were also the crooners, Frank Sinatra being the most popular, but in 1949 or 1950, a phenomenal, successful crooner burst into the scene. This was Johnny Ray, the Elvis of his time. He was an amazing sensation for a couple of years. Although I've always liked Sinatra's music, he has never been my favorite singer. The same goes for Bing Crosby, who was another of the most popular recording artists. My favorite singers of the forties were Frankie Lane, Dinah Shore, Perry Como, and of course, Johnny Ray; with the Glen Miller Orchestra being my favorite big band. And just as has the scent of the seasons, the music of today has also changed drastically. To me, much of today's music is just noise and garbled lyrics.

CHAPTER 8

THE CHILDHOOD YEARS

I was born on November 9, 1936 in Del Rio, Texas. This event having occurred at 8:35 AM, and according to a perpetual calendar, I was born on a Monday. Because of my father's line of work, principally sheep shearing and general ranch work, which at times kept him away for months at a time, it was to be two months before he saw me for the first time.

The little house we lived in when I was born is still there, on the corner of Cortinas St. and Barrera Ave., the address being 312 Cortinas St. I was the last of eleven children but only knew of eight until, as a young adult, I learned of three siblings that had died in infancy. Of the five and a half years we lived at this house, I have very few memories. I believe that my oldest sister, Herminia, (Minnie) was married at this time and was not living with us. I have no memories of my two oldest brothers, Jose and Bernabe, through this time. My oldest brother, Jose, was also married, while Bernabe was in the Philippines during World War ll. I became aware of these two brothers only after we moved a few blocks away, to what I have always called "home," as this is where my childhood memories were built, at 610 Esquivel St.

My brother Jose and sister Elida (Currie) were born in Rocksprings, Texas. It was here that my father met my mother around 1915. Another sister, Epifania (Fane), was born in Johnson City, not far from Rocksprings. The rest of us were born in Del

Rio, and I am under the belief that the youngest of my sisters, Eloisa, "Locha," and I, were the only ones born in a hospital. Before continuing, I may as well get my sibling's nicknames out of the way. Chronologically, the second oldest brother, Bernabe, was known as *Chato*; the oldest sister Herminia, was known as *Minnie*; the second oldest sister, Epifania, was known as *Fane*; the next oldest sister, Elida is known as *Currie*; the third oldest of my brothers, Adolfo Jr., was known as *Dofo*, and the youngest of my sisters, Eloisa, was known as *Locha*.

At the time I was born and throughout most of my childhood, we were as poor as most families in our community. Being a child during the forties, and having had such an amazing upbringing, made being poor less noticeable, in fact, I was simply not aware of what poverty was. The first five years of my life took place at that house, on the corner of Cortinas St. and Barrera Ave. The house was of rectangular shape with the back facing Barrera Ave. on the northeast side, the front faced southeast, parallel to Cortinas St., with the landlord's house across from ours, with a large, bare dirt yard in between; I remember the floors in our house being dirt floors as well.

While I have some fond and early memories of those first years, the latter childhood years, while living on Esquivel St., prevail stronger in nostalgia and poignancy. This is certainly understandable since I was older then, and the world of friendships opened up. Still, I have a few memories of my childhood at the Cortinas address. Both houses were just blocks away from each other, and both close to the San Felipe Creek, with the Cortinas house a mere three blocks away. I remember one day, after a little summer rain, I was playing by the side of the house in a mud puddle, when two women came by asking if my mother was home. I was not yet talking at the time and all I would say was "Mamá." Then they asked, "What is your mother's name?" I kept repeating "Mamá" which was the only name by which I knew my mother. They found this to be amusing and giggled as they walked past me and around to the front of the house.

Although I was not yet able to speak at the time, I do remember the incident, I don't know why I remember it, but that is the very first memory I have of the Cortinas house, or of any thing, as a matter of fact.

During this early part of my childhood, I remember my mother sprinkling the floor of the house to keep the dust down after which she would sweep it smooth. She would also do this to the yard in front of the house. Throughout the San Felipe barrio, few yards had lawns and to this day I remember the scent of the wet dirt whenever my mother watered it down, or after a light rain. Even to this day, whenever there is a light rain, the scent of nostalgia reins.

Three short blocks up on Barrera, from the corner of Cortinas, is the San Felipe Creek, this, the heart and soul of Del Rio and the mother of my childhood memories. Barrera ends at a corner with Bridge St., which parallels the creek. Across Bridge St. is an open space that goes right up to the bank of the creek. One block before Bridge St., Barrera crosses De La Rosa, which, turning left one block south, tees with Taini to the east, and Johnson to the west. Less then a block from this tee, on Johnson, is the legendary bridge *El Puente Del Martillo*, that bridge where someone was bludgeoned to death.Back where Barrera Ave. tees with Bridge Street, and across Bridge Street, one walks onto the open space of land banking the San Felipe Creek. Along this part of the creek, the water is very deep; several boys are known to have drowned here.

To the left of this section of deep water, and less than half a block from it, is a narrow dam known as la presa, or dam. The full length of the dam is not quite the length of a football field and covers a tributary of the creek on the far side. Across this dam, is the canal that I tried to jump over, without success. From the deep side of the dam, the water cascades down about four feet to a much shallower part of the creek, not far from *El Puente Del Martillo*. Walking across the dam, or as far as one could, was a favorite challenge to teenagers and some of the braver younger kids. The dam was fairly narrow, as I mentioned, and very slippery with moss. The challenge was to walk across this portion of the dam, against the force of the cascading water, without falling over. I didn't try this until I was a little older; I don't remember ever making it.

In this area of the creek, that is, where the water cascaded down from the dam, we used to fish using a net. The water in this area was deep enough to swim in, but no more than waist-high. The net we used was usually a gunnysack that we split across the back, and along one of the sides, thus creating a longer net. With one of my friends holding one end of the sack down as far as possible, and I, likewise, holding the other end, we dragged the sack towards the bank and then scooped it up. We always caught some fish and occasionally, a crawdad or two. Sometimes we went "caving," that is mano-a-mano, reaching down into the crevices along the bank with our bare hands and sometimes trapping a fish, while other times, a crawdad would "catch" us by a finger and thusly, we would painfully bring it out. Today I marvel at the size of the crawdads we used to catch; they were some eight inches long, tail to head…and good eating, too!

While living at the Cortinas house, I remember one time walking back home on Barrera Ave. from that open space along Bridge St. with my sisters Currie and Locha and my brother, Dofo. I think it was my sister Currie who was carrying a turtle; I do remember Dofo carrying an eel. Somewhere, I had heard that depending on the color of the turtle's belly, the turtle was either eatable or not. I do remember that the underside of this turtle was yellow. I do not remember, however, that we ate the turtle or the eel, although I would think that's why they were brought home.

I watched with great interest as my brother peeled the skin off the eel and then hung it out to dry on the clothesline, probably for a belt. Another fond (they all were) memory that I cherish during this time is of the times I used to go wading on Barrera after a summer or spring rain. The street was unpaved (still is) and full of good-size chuckholes at the time; this resulted in nice, cool and enjoyable "swimming" holes for a child of four or five. Boy, how I remember wading in those rainwater puddles! Some were actually deep enough for a little belly flop!

By the time I was five or six, I enjoyed playing baseball. One late afternoon, my sister Locha and I were taking turns at bat…a one-on-one game. I had her chasing that softball all over the large, and virtually, vacant yard. As darkness began to ascend, mother called us in for dinner. By this time I was way ahead on the score and as we were walking across the yard, my sister, who was two years older than I, took her frustrations out on me. She lashed at me with open hands, slapping me silly about face and head. I screamed like a pig and started crying, more in anger than in pain. I yelled, "You cut me!" She put her hand on my face to make sure, and feeling the warm tears, she thought it was blood! She pleaded with me not to tell; there was no damage, I was just a spoiled little brat. Could her outrage have been on account of my taunting her? Naw!

In a recent visit to Del Rio, I went to this corner where my life began. My daughter, Ruby, had asked me to bring her a vile of dirt from each of the places where I had lived. I knocked on the door of the main house and this elderly lady answered. I told her of my mission and she asked me in and took me to the backyard to gather my dirt. Having explained the reason for the dirt and the fact that I had been born while living here, she invited me to go in and "revisit" the place of my earliest childhood.

The main house had been remodeled and made bigger, but the house where I was born was still the same simple rectangle, still facing the same way in relation to the main house, just as I remembered it. As soon as I stepped into the front room, I had this inner feeling of going back to my childhood. The front room appeared to be just as when we lived there, it was a combination kitchen and front room, and this is what I was seeing, in my temporary emotional retreat, back in time. It was a very strong feeling, a very real and emotional deja vu.

Another memory of the Cortinas house has to do with bats,

which were very common in Del Rio. These little "winged" mice used to come out in the evenings to feed on mosquitoes and other flying insects. One evening, one of these little critters got into the house, which was also a common occurrence. With that trusty broom in her hands, my mother chased the bat back and forth throughout the house, swatting at it, but to no avail; it was too shifty. Eventually, the bat flew towards the open door and took off…like a bat out of hell!

Directly across Barrera, there was a little mom and pop grocery store that holds a lasting memory of my childhood. This lingering memory is of a very tall avocado tree that towered in the yard, behind the store, just over the fence, on Barrera. Each time we passed by this tree on the way to the creek, I would look up in awe at its branches, hanging way up high. I was completely fascinated by the dark, green fruit dangling from the branches. It is because of this particular memory that I have always wanted to grow an avocado tree in California, but have yet to accomplish.

The spirit throughout America during the forties was one of honor, pride and respect. The honor and the pride we had in our country were very strong then, as was the respect for the law, and for our elders, in general. The respect we had for our teachers, somehow had a different 'feel" to it; it was stronger, in a way, then the general respect we held for others. Such was the social ambiance of the day. The strongest of all, and the most profound form of respect, of course, was that for our parents; this respect was absolute, as natural as breathing.

There are four principal chapters that have shaped my life: my childhood in Del Rio, my school years, and the births of my son and my daughter and, within the last nine years, the birth of my three grandchildren. Through these four chapters of my life, those surviving, childhood friends of mine have also left their notch on what has been a wonderful life.

Poverty was high during the period of the thirties and early forties, this due to the lingering after-effects of the Great Depression of 1929 and that of World War Two. Like so many other small towns through these times, Del Rio found it hard to recover and was among one of the poorest. As poor as we were, I repeat, I enjoyed a very rich childhood. I do remember going with my mother to pick up relief foodstuff somewhere in town. I remember taking a little wagon with us to carry the "stuff" and I like to think that it was a Radio Flyer wagon, which was common then. A few years ago, I bought a vintage Radio Flyer wagon at an antique shop, and ironically, according to the shop records, it was made in 1936, the year I was born. As to the Relief Program, The one item we old timers still talk about is the white butter batch that was handed out along with the packets of yellow food coloring. My sisters had the chore of kneading this into what would eventually look like butter. In spite of these bleak times, I didn't realize the significance; I was too young to understand and too busy being a kid.

Records show that on September of 1942, we moved to 610 Esquivel Street, which, as I mentioned earlier, is very close to the Cortinas house. The Esquivel house is no longer there; my sister, Minnie, had it moved several years ago to one of the lots my father left us. It is still there, on one of these lots, bleached white, with the front door lopsided, but still there. Last time I saw it, it was full of antique furniture and other collectibles my sister had acquired through the years. Minnie acquired this property through her marriage to Manuel Sanchez, who was killed early on, during World War Two. I remember Manuel as being a good-looking man and a very nice man. He and my sister had only one child, my niece Elsa, who still lives in Del Rio; she is my link in Del Rio concerning my childhood friends and special events. Elsa is now a grandmother and has two sons and several grandchildren, all of them living in California. One memory I have of her father, Manuel, is of a time when he took Minnie and me to his family's little dairy farm. The dairy was located on the southern part of Del Rio known as "Las Viñas" or " the vines," that area fronting the Rio Grande and traversed by the San Felipe Creek. Being along the San Felipe Creek and its proximity to the

51

Rio Grande, Las Viñas is still a lush-green and fertile area. What I remember of this trip to the dairy, besides the excitement of being out in the "country" and seeing farm animals, is that I got to see them milk one of the cows and was given a glass of fresh, sweet milk.

On Esquivel Street, the little house we lived in had a front room that protruded towards the street, with the front yard extending no more than ten feet from the curb. Behind this front room was the kitchen, and to the right of the kitchen, was a bedroom where my four sisters slept. I can't imagine now, how all of us fit in that little house. I remember one night my sister Locha and I were sent to bed, and we soon engaged in a pillow fight. My mother came in and warned us to behave and to go to bed. After a few minutes of "behavior," the pillow fight resumed. My mother, once more, called out to us to behave, this time in a more stern voice. Once more, we settled down for a few minutes and then continued our mayhem. This time, the door swung open and my mother stood there threatening us. In shock fear, I anticipated her to say, "Are you going to obey me?" Instead, she said, "Are you going to behave?" Startled, I immediately interrupted her with a reply of "No!" This made her and my sister laugh, and realizing what I had said, I started to laugh too. This time we did go to bed.

We had a wood burning stove in the kitchen that I believe my mother brought with her on the first journey to California; I know she did bring her Singer sewing machine. We didn't have indoor plumbing, so water had to be brought in and heated it up as required for the various uses. As for bathroom facilities, we had that familiar outhouse that was a common "amenity" throughout most of the community. We also didn't have refrigeration in this little house. One of my on-going duties during this part of my childhood consisted of helping my father gather the wood he had chopped, and bring it into the kitchen. Another duty was to, periodically, go to the ice plant, taking my little red wagon with me and bringing home chunks of ice for the icebox. Today, I wonder if the ice plant workers didn't purposely drop the huge blocks of ice off the conveyors, knowing full well the need of the community in which, they, themselves lived.

In my research on Del Rio, I found a photograph of my great-grandfather, Nazario Hernandez in the Whitehead Museum, La Hacienda publication. The photograph also shows my great-grandmother, Florencia Balboa Hernandez, along with three of their children standing in the foreground of the ice plant. My great-grandfather used to work at the old ice plant, and on this day, his little family had come to bring him his lunch.

Along the railroad tracks and below the conveyors, way up above us, we would stand back as the men sent block after block of ice along the conveyor. It was just a matter of time before one of the blocks would collide with a stalled line and the pieces would come crashing down, along with the larger parts being thrown over by the workers. From the many large pieces on the ground, each kid would take his quota and head home; that's the way it was during my childhood.

My mother was a small woman, never reaching above five feet in height. But what a heart! It is she to whom I am forever indebted for giving me such a good life, for teaching me to be more patient, more compassionate, and wiser. She was very loving, very kind, and very compassionate towards others. She handled the discipline when such was required, which was seldom, simply due to our devotion and respect for her. My mother was the best cook ever! This is something that every mother's son will say, and justifiably so.

There are no meals like mother's home cooking. She passed this trait on to two of my sisters, Fane, the second oldest, and to Locha, the youngest of the girls. They, in turn, have passed it on to my nieces. I remember helping my mother clean a batch of pinto beans in preparation for the cooking process. To this day, I don't know where those little pebbles and tiny dirt clots came from. After the cleaning, she would rinse the batch in a pot and drain them; now the beans were ready. She would then put them in the pot with just enough water and set it on the wood stove. How she knew how many beans to the batch, or how much water to the pot, I'll never know. At some point in time, my father would put in his culinary touch; he would put a thick slab of bacon on top of the beans. This not only salted the beans, but also gave them a darn, good flavor. From the freshly cooked pot of beans, my mother would serve us a portion along with a couple of fried eggs, fried potatoes and homemade tortillas. From the pot of "whole" made beans, my mother would make mashed, or "refried" beans for a later meal. This was pretty much our daily staple, along with rice, oatmeal, cream of wheat, Post Toasties or rice pudding, any of which we had for breakfast.

Almost on a daily basis, my father would buy "pan de dulce" or sweet bread, from a vendor who came by every morning. This Mexican pastry was a must, along with a morning cup of hot coffee; still is. Similarly, we had two bottles of milk delivered periodically. My sister Currie and I were usually more anxious than the others for the arrival of the milk. As soon as we heard the milkman's arrival, we would rush outside to get to the milk bottles first, this so that we'd have first dibs at the cream, which was right off the top. This ritual was more than just a treat; it was a game to see who would get to the cream first. Have I mention that we were poor? Well, we were, but we ate beautifully.

The homemade tortillas were especially a treat. I have never had tortillas as good as those made by my mother. Occasionally, I used to watch her make them. She would take just the right amount of flour, and whatever other ingredients needed, put in some water and start kneading the mixture, adding flour, lard and more water, as required. Once she had the right amount to the right consistency, she would take a small amount in her hand and mold it into a biscuit-size bun. This she would place onto a wooden board, and with a wooden roller, commence the ritual of converting these little round buns into almost perfect, circular tortillas, eight inches or so in diameter. Here again, I don't understand how she knew how much of each ingredient it took to make a certain amount of tortillas, to feed us all! One part I remember of this tortilla-making process, is that, inevitably, she would wind up with a tiny amount of dough left. This, she would roll into a circular shape, just like the regular size tortillas, and make me my very own mini-tortilla. What a treat that was for me!

My father was not a tall man; he was of median height, five feet ten inches, at the most. He was not a fat man either, but had a little rotund middle, possibly that slab of bacon and my mom's good cooking. He was a very stoic man, very logical. He would point out a danger to us, such as a red-hot stovetop, and vividly explain the consequences if we were to touch this top. Thereafter, he would leave it up to us to find out just what he meant. On the other hand, I don't remember him playing any kind of games with any of us, nor spending any father and child time with us, one-on-one, such as learning to ride a bike or flying a kite for the first time. Just like hand-me-down clothes, he would depend on the older siblings with helping the younger ones grow up. This was understandable, as the absolute, primary objective of the husband and father was to work, and work was hard to come by in those days, which accounted for his regular absences from Del Rio, therefore, the lack of time for us.

As mentioned in a previous chapter, whenever my father was displeased with any one of us, either because of misconduct or lack of help around the house, he would not direct his concern at us; he would, in our presence, voice his concern to my mother. "I see the yard hasn't been watered!" or "It would be nice to see the girls helping you with the dishes!" These are the type of comments he would make, his way of telling us to "get with it!" My mom would console him by telling him that she would make sure that the "chore" would be taken care of "after breakfast" or "after dinner."

Both my mother and father enjoyed gardening. We didn't have much of a yard in the way of landscaping, but they took pride in planting flowers and vegetables. In the summer, we would all sit outside in the evenings and enjoy eating watermelon that had been grown by them. I also remember sleeping outside on hot summer night, this requiring some kind of netting to keep out the mosquitoes. The back yard also served as a gathering place for relatives, friends and neighbors. The grown ups visited and we young ones ran around, riding our broomstick horse. One "horse" I was really proud of, was a saw bench on which I put some padding and a rolled up towel on the front and on the back, thus forming a "saddle." How that horse could run, and for hours, too! There was one shade tree in the back yard from which I used to shoot a lot of birds with my slingshot, something that I wish I hadn't done. This same tree also served as a clothes hanger for my sister Currie's bathing suit; that is until one day when she went to retrieve it and as she reached for the swimsuit, she jumped back, screaming in horror; there were several scorpions nearby; these are were very popular in Del Rio.

One memory that is hard to forget occurred one year when I stayed in Del Rio while my parents had gone back to California. You have to remember that during our childhood, we could be any one of a number of super heroes. Most of the time I was Gene Autry or Wild Bill Elliot, AKA Red Ryder; other times I was Tarzan, Captain America or Captain Marvel. On this one particular day, I was Superman. I had a large towel for a cape, this, draped around my neck and tied at the corners with a piece of rope. I really was Superman, running around the yard so that my "cape" flew up behind me. I would run and jump up as high as I could, throwing my arms up, pointing to the sky, ready to take off. Well, off to the side, in the back yard, was a chicken coop. This looked like a tall enough building from which to jump, so I made my way up to the top and stood there surveying my surroundings. Then, "up, up and away!" I leaned forward, as if diving into a swimming pool, and jumped off. Somehow, my cape got caught in the mesh wire of the chicken coop. I hung upside down, looking at the ground not far from my face, but not for long. My sister Minnie saw me hanging there and panicked.

She came running up to the chicken coop and quickly untangled the towel from the wire mesh. "Kerpow!" I went straight down and got myself a bloody nose. I know "kerpow" is a comic book sound from the Batman series, but you get the point. Nevertheless, I wouldn't trade even that part of my childhood, for nothing.

It was probably around this time that my "gang' pulled a "heist." Two cousins of mine, another neighborhood kid whose name I don't remember, and I pulled the great-neighborhood-store robbery. Our community was dotted with little "Mom and Pop" stores, and one of these was not too far from where I lived on Esquivel. The four of us went in, and while one of us was actually buying something, the others were pocketing gum sticks. Most of these stores had these bins with a lift-up glass door in which a variety of candies and the single sticks of gum were stored. After the "heist," we ran to my house, where in the back yard, we "divvied up" the loot. I think the average age between the four of us was just under six. As wrong as this was, and still is, all four of us wound up being upstanding citizens. One of my cousins wound up being an educator, teaching Algebra in high school.

A childhood friend, Joe Rodriguez, and I, also share a couple of memorable, and humorous incidents that occurred while living at the Esquivel house. One of these also took place in the back yard, this one long after my superman fiasco. But first, it is necessary that I interject a little story here, concerning a very special dog.

There were two main routes I could take to school every day. The most direct way required that I pass by this house where a mongrel bulldog lived. He terrorized me every day! As soon as I approached the house, whether it was going to, or coming from school, he would start barking viciously while charging the cyclone fence at full speed. I feared the day when he would break through. Well, one day I was really frightened as I approached the house on my way home; I didn't hear the dog bark! I always walked on the far side of the street, and on this particular day

I didn't see nor hear the dog. Talk about the hairs on you neck standing up! I was sure he was loose. I ran home, as fast as I could, and once I turned onto my street, I felt safe, so I slowed down. Just as I got to the house before ours, I froze in shock at seeing the dog sitting on our small porch, the same dog that had been terrorizing me all year! Fortunately, my brother, Dofo came out of the house at that moment and said, "Look what we got!" Somehow, and it was just meant to be, the owners of the dog had given it to my brother. From that moment on, Gordo became my best friend and the best watchdog I have ever had. I never asked under what circumstances we got that dog.

Now, I go back to the incident in the backyard. On this particular day, Joe and I were playing cowboys. We had a lariat that we would twirl above our heads and take turns chasing each other with the objective of "roping" the bad guy. I was chasing Joe around the house a couple of times, passing by Gordo while he rested in the backyard. I roped Joe and at that point, we switched places and Joe took the rope. Well, as soon as he started chasing me, Gordo jumped up and went after Joe, nipping him in the butt! Joe wasn't hurt, but we stopped playing at that point, and I felt a sense of pride for Gordo; I realized that he was just protecting me.

Another incident, again concerning, Joe and this time, a cousin of his happened some time later. My mother had sent my brother Dofo and me to go to her niece's house and retrieve a "tina" or tin washtub, in which my mother washed the clothes. This niece of my mother's, whom I refer to as my aunt, lived two blocks down and one block east, from us. The corner where we would turn towards my aunt's house was a vacant lot with a visibly, well-used path, kiddy-corner through it. Otherwise, it was filled with mesquite trees, sagebrush and wild grass, typical community landscape.

Blocking our way through this lot was Joe's older brother, Lee, an older, and a younger cousin of theirs, and of course, Joe. "Where are you going?" Joe's brother asked my brother. "We're going to pick up a tina over at my aunt's," replied my brother. "No you're not!" replied Lee. "Not unless your brother fights my brother and my cousin!" Well, as I've said before, we kids could be any one of many heroes at any given time and I, for some reason, wasn't scared of the situation. So in "defending" my brother, I took Joe and his cousin on, both of them being my age. Joe and I lunged at each other, falling to the ground, with me landing on top. Now, call it instinct, common sense, or just plain luck, but I anticipated his cousin to take advantage of the situation and jump on top of me. Well, just in the nick of time, I rolled off of Joe and his cousin landed on top of him! I immediately jumped on top of both of them, at which point the older boys, amused, took us apart. All was well and we were all friends again, and my brother and I were allowed to continue. Joe, his older brother and the older cousin turned out to be close friends of ours, with Joe and I keeping in touch now and then through adulthood.

I lost track of his younger cousin, but several years ago, I ran into Joe at a popular, Del Rio crowd hangout here in San Jose. We were both middle age by this time, with Joe a pretty good-sized boy; he looked to be about six feet two, weighing about two hundred and ten pounds. Enjoying a cold one, the subject of that "brawl" when we were kids, came up. He said he and his cousin spoke of it occasionally, and that his cousin had told him in recent years, "I'd like to see Ruben try it now!" No thanks! Joe told me at that time, that his cousin was even bigger than he. We laughed and I told Joe that at this point in time, I couldn't whip him alone even if he had one arm tied behind his back, maybe even both. I'm sure that was a pretty fair statement.

Concerning my dog, Gordo, which by this time we had claimed each other as loyal, trusting friends, one day, a couple of friends and I were sitting on the sidewalk just three houses down from my house. This was at the intersection of Esquivel and Gillis, a main road that leads east to Eagle Pass. A block west from this intersection was one of those little mom-and-pop grocery stores, this one owned by an uncle of one of the childhood friends, Henry Davis. Coming from the store towards us, was this man carrying a bag of groceries. As he approached us, we kids immediately got out of the way; Gordo did not. The man ignored Gordo's growling and continued to go past him. Gordo bit the man on the ankle, causing the man to drop his groceries. I quickly called Gordo back as the man, just as quickly, picked up his groceries. As he left hurriedly, he called back, over his shoulder, sayint that he was goin to call the police. Yhis is the last memory i have og Gordo.

In all directions from Gibbs down to Main Street, and for the most part, all around the community from the west banks of the San Felipe Creek, the streets were paved. The houses were well kept and had landscaping that complimented their appearance. Whenever we went downtown, we walked on the sidewalks along this part of town; and all the homes in this section had driveways and in-door plumbing. This is how those of us who lived in the San Felipe community, viewed this section of Del Rio, a dire contrast to our San Felipe barrio. The contrast was vivid. Most of the streets throughout the San Felipe community, east of San Felipe Creek, were not paved; the houses are older and much smaller. Outhouses dotted this community, each outhouse being located at a given, far corner of the backyard. Sidewalks were rare, and instead of lawns, most yards were bare, with no vegetation other than one or two native trees, a few planted shrubs and in most cases, a little spot for a vegetable garden somewhere along the sides of the yard.

Highway 277, one of the few principal roads in Del Rio, makes a horseshoe loop beginning at the border with Mexico at the south end of town, having its rounded peak on the north side, where it crosses over the San Felipe Creek. Here, it loops southeast out of town towards Eagle Pass. This highway was paved, of course, and there were four or five other principal streets that were paved, but for the most part, the streets in the San Felipe barrio were narrow, unpaved and full of chuckholes. I use the past tense here because I am writing about my childhood, a childhood that took place in this community over sixty years ago. San Felipe covers that portion of Del Rio east of the creek. I find it painful that this part of Del Rio has been so neglected. The city itself has improved, but not much, certainly not sixty years worth, and throughout the San Felipe community, there are still streets that remain unpaved, the same weathered, narrow streets I walked on sixty years ago!

I do not remember the move to Esquivel Street, and in fact, it was only recently, during my research, that I realized that we had lived at the Cortinas house for as long as we had. I had always thought of having lived there only to the age of five or less and even thought of the Esquivel house as my first home. In spite of this, the chuckhole wading memories and the avocado tree on Barrera Ave. have always been there, in the canyons of this grateful mind of mine.

Winters were very cold and as mentioned, poverty prevailed throughout most of Del Rio during this period of my life. This, I remember of my childhood and yet, I treasure the memories and consider that time to have been one of the richest moments in my life. The memories involve many friends with whom I experienced them; I still see a few of these friends on my visits to Del Rio. Among my childhood friends, of course, there were also a few girls by whom I was smitten, these starting in the second grade and on through the second semester in the eighth-grade, the first semester having been at Orchard Elementary, in San Jose, California.

There were several close friends with whom I played many of those nostalgic games that kids played in those days. However, there were three friends in particular, with whom I spent most of my time, and whom I have always considered as my best friends. One was Teno Flores who still lives on Bridge Street, and whom I see each time I visit Del Rio. His back yard is directly above the banks of the San Felipe Creek. Another one of these three friends is Richard Perez, who also lived on Bridge Street, a few

61

houses down from Teno. Richard's back yard also banked the San Felipe Creek and on one side of the yard, there was an open lot that provided us with beautiful adventures. This stretch of land was well treed with mesquite, sagebrush and other indigenous vegetation. On it, close to Richard's house, we built a hideout by digging a rectangular hole big enough and deep enough for us to sit in. The roof for our hideout was made up of tree limbs over which we placed cardboard or tin sheets that we then covered with dirt, leaving a small entrance at one end. Inside our hideout, we lit candles and took some snacks in with us. Little did I know that generations before ours, people in early San Felipe lived in similar shelters.

The creek and the surrounding terrain gave us many adventures. The outdoors, or frontier, was easily accessible to us kids. Beside the swimming and the fishing, we also hunted mourning doves all around this terrain. Almost any day, it was common for us to shoot a few of these doves with our slingshots. We would feather and gut them, build a fire right on the spot and barbecue them on a stick. I remember the meat being very tasty. We were probably nine or ten years old at the time. One such shooting involving a mourning dove took place out of Teno's backyard. Down along the bank from Teno's, were several large threes and on one of these, I saw the head of the dove sticking out of the nest. The tree was so far and the target so small, there was no way I thought I could hit it, but I did; it was a marble I used. Besides the shear shock and regret, Teno had asked me just before not to shoot doves around his house as they fed these birds. How awful is that?

During those years, Richard's father was a well-known police Officer and a well-liked man. I remember him taking Richard and me down to the bank of the creek and letting us shoot his snub-nose handgun at empty cans. The cans were a short distance and right in front of us, but we couldn't hit them because of the recoil. Richard now lives in San Antonio and I also got to see him there a few years ago.

The third of these three friends, and whom I considered my best friend through those childhood years, is Tony Treviño. He too, lives in San Antonio now. A few years ago, I contacted a title company in Del Rio on some property my father left us. Ironically, the person with whom I was speaking happened to be Lisa Treviño, who, to my joyous surprise, happens to be Tony's niece. As a result, I was able to get in touch with Tony after more than thirty years, when he and his small family had visited me here in San Jose, in the seventies.

There were so many outdoor activities I enjoyed with my childhood friends. One simple activity we all enjoyed was making a sailboat out of a sheet of paper. During the summers or early spring rains, we would fold this sheet in such a way that by pulling the center of it outwardly after the proper folding, a sailboat would be created. When the rain stopped, since the streets weren't paved, rivulets would run for blocks and we would turn our sailboats loose, in front of our house and watch them go as far as the "river" took them. We followed our little sailboats for a block or so and brought them back, only to turn them loose again. What a simple and enjoyable pastime that was. I am sure that all kids in Del Rio, and surely, those of other small towns, enjoyed this simple pastime. Another, simpler pastime was taking a discarded bicycle rim and a piece of thick wire with properly folded "U" at the front end, thus guiding the rim as we pushed it around, as if walking a dog on a leash; most kids did this.

Playing marbles was another pastime, and also a sort of "Daycare Center" for our parents, as sometimes we'd be gone for most of the day. On any given day, at any of the various marble games we played, we would either go home with more marbles than we had taken, or with less, depending on our skill and on lady luck. One simple game we played involved just two players. One player would toss his marble a certain distance out of harms way, and the second player would then follow cautiously, with his marble. The objective of the game was sort of a cat and mouse game; each player chased the other while trying not to get too close to the other player's marble, less he gave the opponent a clear shot at his marble. The first one to hit his opponent's marble was the winner of the other's marble.

Another, one-on-one game, involved a little slight of hands that required a little trickery at the very last moment before delivering the marbles into a hole. Each player would put up a certain number of marbles and each, in turn, would take the marbles and cupping them in one hand, cleverly drop them into a small, shallow hole. With acquired skill, and just the right sway of the wrist, and maybe a flick of the fingers at just the right moment, the marbles would be dropped in an easy, swinging motion. The hole was about three inches in diameter and maybe two inches deep, tapering towards the bottom. Prior to dropping the marbles into the hole, the player would call out either even or odd, and these are the marbles he would keep, while the second player would keep the remainder.

There was one marble game we played that involved scribing a big circle on the ground, about a foot and a half in diameter. Each player put in an equal number of marbles inside the circle and then, each one in turn, would shoot his marble into the circle and try to knock as many marbles out as possible, this while trying to keep his shooter in the circle. This was the objective: to stay in the circle, because as long as one's shooter stayed in the circle, one kept shooting. Thus, those who were good at putting a backspin on the "shooter" marble, would stay inside the circle for quite a while. I have a cousin, Rolando Lomas, who was the best shooter I ever saw play. There were times when, once he was in the circle, he would just about clear all the marbles. He had a mean backspin and control of his shooter. Each player kept however many marbles he shot out of the circle.

One other marble game that comes to mind required five shallow holes, with four holes in a square pattern and the fifth hole in the middle of the square pattern. Each hole was about three inches in diameter at the top, and again, tapered somewhat, towards the bottom. From a set distance, the first player would aim his shooter marble at the first hole, again, being cautious where he landed, as the next player would try to knock the other player's marble away from the hole. And so it went, each player in turn, trying to get his marble in each of the four outer holes, when, then, and only then, could he go for the middle fifth hole. All the while, there was the tension and excitement, hoping nobody knocked you away in the process. Once a player made it to the fifth hole, he was free to go around and "finish" off each of the other players before they could get into the fifth hole. The winner would win all the marbles bet by each player.

A lot of our time was spent "hunting" either with our slingshots, or with our trusty Red Ryder, Daisy BB gun. Most of us were very good sharpshooters, simply because we did this day after day during the summertime. Our hunting grounds were vast and within a matter of a few blocks from the residential area. Surrounding the San Felipe barrio was a vast, open range of sagebrush, mesquite trees and other shade trees, but mostly mesquite and cacti. This range provided good hunting grounds for our game, namely different type of birds, many jackrabbits, and other critters such as lizards and snakes. There was one type of lizard that was understood to be off limits; we did not shoot at this particular one. Somehow, this lizard, the horned toad, seemed to exude a "scary" aura. This short, stubby lizard had "horns" on its head and a spiny, or scaly back; it almost looked like a medieval "monster." For whatever reason we respected this lizard, we still found enjoyment in watching it sit perfectly still, by an anthill, and swiftly, dart out its tongue at its targeted meal. While he enjoyed his meal, he was totally aloof of the ants crawling all over his head and body; his eyes would just blink whenever an ant crawled over them. Perhaps that is why we respected this lizard; he was our own backyard, anteater.

The one, wild game that we seldom pursued, although it was in abundance, was the jackrabbit; this critter was too elusive for us. We seldom came across snakes, so our primary game was a variety of birds, some very beautiful birds. I have so regretted having shot so many of them, although some were eatable; the others were just plain "sport." The eatable birds, as mentioned, were the mourning doves, or turtledoves as they were otherwise called. In Spanish, we called them, "tortolitas." In my defense, shooting birds in the forties was such a part of childhood life that I'm sure this adventure was happening in many small towns across America; I have to believe this.

When I got my own Red Ryder Daisy BB gun, it was a most satisfying, childhood dream come true. I remember it coming with a practice target that had a bell behind it; if the target was hit, one could hear when the "bulls eye" was actually hit. I'm sure that nationwide, it was every kid's dream to have one of these trusty rifles. Unfortunately, this "toy" was also used to kill innocent birds. To this day I can't explain why we did it, nor can I express enough, how much I regret it. In later years, I found the Texas State bird to be the Mockingbird. During my childhood, I didn't think of the Mockingbird any differently than the rest of the birds and they too, were fair game through that "v" notch at the end of the BB gun barrel. I wish I had known the high status of this bird, I would have spared them it as I did the horned toad.

Today, we have a couple of Mockingbirds hanging out in our backyard, here in San Jose. I wonder if they came all the way from Texas just to haunt me; they are sure melodiously loud! And the time they choose to start their serenade is usually around 3 o'clock in the morning! There have always been two birds of special interest to me; these are the Robin and the Cardinal. I tried many times to capture either one of these two birds but fortunately, without success; else wise, I'd have another bird regret. Today, I don't see that many Robins here in California, and I have yet to see a Cardinal since my childhood in Del Rio.

Probably the pastime that took most of our growing-up years was softball. Baseball, during this time, was truly the American pastime and we used to play softball out on the streets, anywhere, anytime. During this period of time, I thought that I would grow up to be either an artist (I have always enjoyed drawing), a lawyer (because of Abraham Lincoln) or a professional baseball player because of Babe Ruth. I read Bob Considine's book on the Babe and saw the William Bendix movie seven times; I used to push my nose up so that I'd have a pug nose like the Babe. My brother-in-law, Pablo Salazar, or "Beaver" as most people know him by, brought me a long, narrow toolbox one day.

Beaver was a carpenter by trade, and this box, most likely, he brought from work. The box was just perfect for a baseball bat to fit in, along with a few baseballs and a couple of old mitts. I used to carry this box with me just about every day during spring and summer, just in case a game of baseball showed up Among my circle of friends, there were some girls who were pretty good baseball players, some better than some of the boys. Among these was my girlfriend, Baby Calderon; she was an excellent hitter and could throw the ball as well as many of the boys.

Two very popular pastimes were yoyos and spinning tops. I wasn't very good at spinning yoyos, nor at spinning tops, whereas, some of the boys in the hood could do "magic" with the yoyos. They could make it spin in place, "walk the dog" and other spins that were very difficult for me. I was a little better at spinning tops, as this required less dexterity. My nephew, Papi (Jose Jr.) could wrap the string around the top of a spinning top and toss it close to ten yards away, where it would land, spinning. Usually, Christmas was the time I got a yoyo or a spinning top. I remember just how much it meant to me to get a brand new, shiny spinning top or yoyo, these, bright green, blue, or red in color. The yoyos, we would enjoy just spinning, but the tops, we would use for destroying a competitor's top. Usually, we would use an old beat up top as the target and our new one as the weapon. Taking turns at each other's target top, we would spin ours, which was actually held with the tip facing up and as we spun it towards the target, the release would flip it over and hopefully, crack the opponent's top in two; that was the objective of the game.

Although the winters were cold in Del Rio, I only remember that year when it snowed enough to build a healthy snowman. Other winters, just the cold of the mornings made walking to school mighty uncomfortable. Most of us kids walked to school with our books and binders tightly tucked under one arm and both hands in our pockets. Those of us who rode bicycles, would have our hands in our pockets (after having mastered the "no hands" riding) and our schoolbooks would be tightly stacked in the bike rack. Some of us wore a woolen cap with earmuffs and we'd all walk with our heads bowed so as not to face the chilly air of those cold, winter mornings. We didn't have school busses and most families didn't have cars, so walking, or riding our bicycles to school, was the ticket.

I mentioned in an earlier chapter that the thing I feared most about winter was the torrential rain and the thunder and lightening that came with it. We didn't have streetlights, so nighttime got awfully dark. I remember nights when, out of curiosity, I would look out the window unto total darkness, when all of a sudden, a huge, jagged bolt of lightening would light up the sky and for a split second, eerily silhouette the houses across the street; this, followed by an enormous thunder blast, made me think the world was ending.

The scariest incident I remember occurred when I was about eleven years old. I was in the hospital recovering from having my appendix removed and my mother was by my bedside. That evening and through the night, we had gotten, not only a heavy torrential rainstorm, but also an unusually heavy hailstorm, with hailstones as big as golf balls, and in some places, as big as a baseball! Above me, the water stains were increasing around the ceiling fan, which was not quite directly above my bed. Outside my room, panic reigned, as nurses wheeled patients and newborn babies from room to room, escaping the leaking water. At this time, I saw the ceiling fan give way, and the water fell on part of my bed. The nurses quickly pushed my bed clear of the leaking spot and it was at this time that my mother knelt down and prayed; she was so frightened, and so was I. The storm soon subsided, but the damage was done. The hospital suffered much damage to the windows and to the roof. Throughout Del Rio automobiles suffered extensive damage; sheep and other animals were hurt or killed. The storm covered areas beyond Del Rio, where similar damages occurred. I have not experienced another hailstorm that powerful since.

It is interesting to note that the day before I was taken to the hospital, I had been out playing with friends in another part of our neighborhood; it was safe to do so in those days. It was dark when I headed home on my bicycle and a little scared going home in the dark, as the cemetery was close to where we had been playing. When I turned onto the dirt driveway of our house, I jumped off the bicycle and ran in as fast as I could. As I was closing the door behind me, I could hear the bicycle crashing into the garage in the backyard. It was later that evening that I felt nauseous and folded over with a severe stomach pain. I was taken to the hospital where it was determined that I needed to have my appendix taken out. The good side of this experience: two of my childhood "sweethearts" came to visit me while I was in the hospital. Incidentally, ether was used in those days to put you out and it smelled like burnt tire to me. I can still sense that smell or "taste" whenever I recall that experience. This incident took place while I was living on Waters Street, where I caught tarantulas.

I mentioned how cold it was in the winter and how our parents bundled us up as warm as possible. One thing that most of us experienced during the school year was wearing a pair of shoes until they were literally falling apart. At first, the first layer of the sole would begin to break through. Through this period, we would begin inserting a piece of cardboard to minimize the impact on the gravel streets. As the break in the sole increased, so did the size of the cardboard. Eventually, the front of the sole would part from the shoe, but we would continue to wear them to school with the inevitable flip-flop of the loose sole. It was at this time that we "qualified" for a new pair of shoes. The old shoes didn't go to waste, though. We would use the tongue for our slingshots, that trusty, friend that offered such a favorite pastime for us. If the sides of the shoes were intact and smooth, we would use them too. This was a very common occurrence in our community and something that we, of that generation, still talk about whenever we chance to meet, unfortunately, usually at someone's funeral.

Some of the best days of my childhood in Del Rio also involved playing street football. When we played football, since none of us kids on the block could afford a real football, we used an empty Bull Durham tobacco pouch, stuffed real tight with sifted dirt. My dad, and other men in our neighborhood smoked Bull Durham, consequently, we always had a "football" to play with.

An evening game we used to play was "kick the can," a kind of hide-and-seek game. The objective of the game, as I recall, involved one player who was "it" chasing after a can that one of the other players had kicked away as far as possible. The "it" player would go out and retrieve the can, thus giving the other players time to scatter and hide. Upon retrieving the can, The "it" player would put it back on the spot from where it had been kicked, and then, careful not to get too far from the it, he would "seek" the other players. Upon spotting a player, he would have to run back to the can and touch it before the player got a chance to kick it away. If the "spotted" player got to the can first, he would kick it away again, this freeing any "found" players. This seems very frustrating to me now.

Other forms of recreation included playing hopscotch, or jacks, with my sister Locha and other kids in the neighborhood. Needless to say I was not good at either one of these, especially at jacks, where my sister Locha would always beat me. Fishing was not only recreational, but it was also a way of bringing food

70

home. Occasionally, we'd sell our catch to neighbors, along the way. As mentioned before, our fishing rods came from the bamboo that grew along the banks of the San Felipe Creek, as did the bait. We used the same kite string for our fishing line, and we usually caught several fish. For the hook, it was very common for us to use bent straight pins or safety pins; we were poor, and we improvised. One very simple pasttime, and again, very common in my childhood, was playing cowboys. For our "spurs", we would stomp on empty tin cans, which would wrap tightly around our shoes, and we'd walk tall, listening to the clank of our "spurs".

As to fishing, one, perhaps hard-to-believe fish story is this: We used to take copper wire from discarded electrical parts and use it as a "roping" fishing line by forming a loop at the front end, creating a "noose". The creek water was very clear; we could easily see the multi-colored pebbles on the bottom as well as the fish. The fish we roped, was a good size fish that we knew as a "sucker fish," of the carp family. It swam with its snout facing down, close to the bottom, scooping its food. Placing the noose some distance ahead of the fish, we'd wait for it to swim into the noose and quickly pull on the line and thus, the fish was "roped." Amazingly, we caught many of these fish in this manner. I tried this in recent years just for the nostalgia, with the help of my childhood friend Teno. I asked him to turn my camcorder on, just in case I got lucky; the fish were too foxy this time.

One fishing experience was my "fish tale", which involved using a safety straight pin for a hook, kite string for the line, and of course, a bamboo fishing pole. I was fishing along a narrow part of the creek not far from the spring's source, and close to the Country Club golf course. The fish just kept biting and I just kept pulling them out! The fish I caught were blue gill, or what I know as perch. I caught fourteen of them, with my simple, crude gear. This is a true story, and I love to tell it.

The abundance of the bamboo along the creek, provided for excellent kite material, although I did use balsa wood, but not too often. Occasionally, I made a hexagonal-shaped kite, which required two long strips approximately twenty-four inches long. These, I crossed in an oblong cross, with the cross being narrower at the top and wider at the bottom. A shorter, horizontal strip was placed across the intersection of the oblong cross, and all three strips were tied tightly at their intersection. Notching the ends of all the strip ends provided for securing string all around the frame, thus providing the hexagonal shape. A "loose" length of string was looped between the two ends at the top of the oblong cross and a longer one between the ends of the horizontal strip. These two loops, when pulled together, provided the center point where the main, "flying" string would be tied. A shorter loop would also be tied between the two ends at the bottom of the oblong cross, this providing for attaching the tail. The final finishing of the kite was the "flying" material used on the frame. Taking a two-page section of a newspaper, preferably the comic's section, I would place the frame on top of the newspaper and notch the newspaper to clear the ends of each bamboo strip. Then, very patiently, I fold the paper around each strip and glued it in place with homemade glue, this made out of flour with just a little water, to make it pasty. For the tail I used strips of any discarded fabric such as tee shirts or, of first choice, strips of cotton sheets; they just don't make kites like that anymore.

More often, I made a simpler kite made of only two strips crossing each other perpendicularly, with the shorter, horizontal member crossing the longer vertical member some distance past the middle. The kite was then finished in similar fashion as the three-strip kite. It was a very common occurrence to have our kites get tangled around telephone lines or get caught up in a tree. Sometimes we were able to salvage the kite by hurling a sling above the kite and around the lead string. The sling was comprised of a piece of string with a rock tied at each end and twirling this sling at our kite, it would wrap itself securely around the string and hopefully, bring the kite down.

There are three incidents concerning my next-door neighbor

and fellow playmate Carlos "Chale" Garza. He is my age and brother to Alica, whose bracelet I found playing that silly game I mentioned earlier. One incident occurred during an Easter Sunday celebration at the State Park. The fifties movie, Picnic reminds me of those family Easter picnics that the entire community celebrated. Anyway, Chale and I were either eight or nine at the time and we were running amuck, chasing each other and jumping over narrow puddles. I was a little faster than Chale, and as we leaped over a puddle, our strides were in unison with my right heel going backwards while his left shin was coming forward. He went down like a rock, writhing in pain; I was more than surprised, I was frightened because Chale was really hurt. In recent years, on a visit to Del Rio, I looked Chale up and visited with him. One of the first things he asked was, "Do you remember when you hit me with your foot?" He reminded me that he had to be taken to the hospital; I didn't remember that. He also showed me the scar. Chale and I shared some other, memorable childhood experiences. One of these involved a minor, dastardly deed. We were out for a walk a few blocks from our houses, just killing time. Walking up the half block to the end of Esquivel St., we turned left on Mclymont St. and walked the three blocks to De La Rosa. At the corner of McLymont and De La Rosa, there was an empty lot filled with the typical vegetation also with a well-worn trail, diagonally crossing the lot. My paternal grandmother's house was adjacent to this lot on the corner of McLymont and Urista, just before De La Rosa, which proved to be of help to me on the fast way back home.

Having cut across the empty lot, we turned south on De La Rosa to Broadbent Ave, a main street that meets up with highway 277 outside of town, on the east side. Coming towards us, on Broadbent Ave, was an older model car. Somehow, and for no good reason at all, we dared each other to throw something in front of the car as it passed by. We each picked up a piece of wood and at the right moment, flung it in front of the car. To our dismay, the car not only came to a stop, but this man got out

73

and started running after us! We turned tail and ran as fast as we could, back-tracking our route. Once again, we cut across the empty lot and as we got to my grandmother's house, I thought to jump up onto the porch, bracing myself against the wall of the house. It worked! I saw the man pass by in full pursuit of Chale. I waited for a while and then slowly made my way home. On Esquivel St., my house was just before Chale's so I went around the far corner of my house to the backyard. From the front yard of Chale's house, I could hear the man complaining and arguing with the Garza family. I learned later, from Chale, that he had hidden under his house and that nothing had come out of this incident. I don't remember if my parents ever found out, I didn't volunteer the information.

Another incident involving Chale had to do with boxing. Although Chale and I never had words or expressed bad feelings towards each other, I was a little scared of Chale. He was the same age as I, but he was heavier and stronger. Looking back on my childhood, I was pretty good at sports, mainly baseball, but I also liked boxing. During this period of time, boxing was very popular in our community. I used to shadow box in the backyard with a pair of boxing gloves I had made myself. These were made of two strips of cloth material stitched together over a pad of foam sponge, or several strips of the same cloth material. I remember leaving the ends of the outer strips hanging out loose and just long enough to wrap them around my hands.

One day, a mutual friend of ours, Henry Davis came by with a real set of gloves. Henry lived around the corner from our street and one block away. He was one of the few kids in our neighborhood whose family had money. As I recall, there were five or six of us on the empty lot, which was just one block up from my house. We decided to have a boxing tournament among us, through a process of elimination. After going through the other challengers, it came down to Chale and me and I was quite concerned. I gave him a bloody nose early in the fight, and as our time limit expired, I was declared the winner, and was I relieved!

I was scared of Chale before, during and after the fight. Chale, understandably, wanted satisfaction and wanted to go another set of rounds. Being scared and aware of his intention, I tried to avoid it, as we had already gone through the tournament, as I pointed out. He insisted we go one more round and since there was an unwritten code among us kids that no one backed down from a challenge or a dare, I agreed. Under this pressure, I said okay, but only if we agreed to only one round. He said okay, and we went at it one more time. Well, the results were the same and this time, I was really glad it was over! Chale kept his word. The group packed it up and we all went our separate ways.

Since Chale and I lived next door to each other, we walked home together. I was carrying my homemade gloves over my shoulder and as we approached my house, Chale brought up going another round. I could just sense his need to get even, and as I said earlier, I was a scared even though I had beaten him twice. I am very sure that in a street fight, Chale would have gotten the best of me. With some trepidation on my part, I relented once more, and we went to my backyard for one more round. I handed him one set of my homemade gloves and while I was putting mine on, Chale quickly threw his to the ground and got me with a bare-fist punch to the jaw, then quickly ran home. Besides being shocked, and in pain, I remember being angry, and not knowing what else to do, I picked up some rocks and threw them at him. One of our friends, who lived directly behind Chale's house, saw what had happened and apparently enjoyed the incident, for he was laughing with pleasure. Although I beat Chale twice in a fair fight, as I stated before, in a real street fight, Chale could have paved any one of our watered-down, gravel streets with me.

As I usually do on my visits to Del Rio, I make it a point to look up childhood friends. Several years ago, on one of these visits, I was able to find where Chale lived, which in fact, was not far from our original Esquivel St. residences. The house I stopped at to ask for him happened to be one belonging to one of his children. It was such a good feeling to meet the children and grandchildren of an old childhood friend of mine. One of the young men directed me to the house next door where Chale happened to live. It was one of his grand kids who walked me over to where Chale was doing some carpentry work in the backyard. What a moment it was, to see this old friend after more than forty years! Chale took me into the house and introduced me to his wife, who served us a glass of welcomed ice tea. One of the first things that Chale brought up was of the time I sent him to the hospital and he even raised his pant leg up to show me the scar he had carried all these years.

There is one childhood friend whom I did not know too well, but he was certainly one of the neighborhood kids; this was Sidney Blanks, a black kid that lived kitty-corner from my close friend, Teno Flores, on the corner of Gillis and Bridge Street. Just west and across the San Felipe Creek from this intersection, is Memo's, a landmark restaurant in Del Rio. The Calderon family, Baby Calderon having been my very first girlfriend, owns the restaurant. Tony Treviño, whom I have always considered my best friend through the childhood years, lived directly across from Memo's.

Both Tony and Teno were closer friends with Sidney, as was Richard Perez, the third of my closest friends and who also lived on Bridge Street. All of these friends of mine went through high school at San Felipe High where Sidney was to be a football star. Tony tells me that Sidney scored every point during a season; that is, he scored the extra points, field goals and the touchdowns! One game that was played in a muddy field, Tony tells me that Sidney took his cleats off and taped his feet and just ran amuck on the playing field. The one story concerning Sidney I find most enjoyable is of an away-from-home game. San Felipe High used to play little towns like Uvalde, Brackettville, Hondo, and several others. At one of these games, Sidney was walking downtown with some of the other players when they met up with a small group of locals, all Mexican-American. One of then, pointing out Sidney, and supposedly suggested to the others that they should work Sidney over before the game. Sidney walked up to this particular kid, and in fluid Spanish, asked the kid why he needed his friends and basically, to take care of business, mano-a-mano! Well that ended the confrontation.

As one of the kids in the San Felipe neighborhood, which was predominantly Mexican-American, Sidney Blanks spoke Spanish every bit as well as we did. He went on to college and was drafted by the Houston Oilers as a running back, a position in which he was very successful. I went to see one of his games in Oakland, California when the Oilers played the Oakland Raiders, and just as half-time was ending, I went along the outside of the field and called out to Sidney in Spanish. I quickly blurted out that I was a childhood friend of Tony, Teno and Richard and asked if he remembered us. He responded, in Spanish, that he did; Sidney is another little bit of Del Rio pride.

There was another, very athletic childhood friend who lived two house down from me, next to Chale's house. His name is Hermilo (Milo) Ledesma. He still lives in the same house and I got to see him briefly, one o my visits to Del Rio.

Milo was one of the kids that played street football with us, but while still in grade school, played organized baseball, at which he excelled. I remember that he could place his hits to any spot on the field, depending on the base the runner was on. Years later, here in San Jose, I met up with Milo in a flag football game, at which he also excelled. My team consisted of a "make-shift" group of friends while Milo was playing with a city league team; Club San Felipe, which I was later asked to join, in fact, right after that game.. While Milo is two, maybe three inches shorter than I am, there was one play in which he made me look bad. Humbleness put aside, I was a darn good player myself, but I was no match for Milo's speed. Playing safety, I was guarding Milo as he went for a long pass. He went by me, but I had all the confidence that I could intercept the pass; after all, he was much shorter than I. Well, I was wrong. Milo went past me and the pass was just over my fingertips and he scored a touchdown. All of us kids in our neighborhood were aware of Milo's athletic prowess, he had the speed and the moves.

The camaraderie was great among us kids in our community. We socialized with each other through so many childhood activities. Our childhood revolved around all those games that kids played in the forties. The social condition in America today is a far cry from the one I experienced during my childhood. It would be inconceivable today for any responsible and caring parent to let their children roam the neighborhood, especially at night. The concerns most parents had when I was a kid were that we might fall off a tree, or off our bikes, or shoot our eye out with our BB gun. Anyway, my childhood was certainly, socially more healthy.

In recent years, here in San Jose, I've run into three childhood friends from Del Rio, and each time we meet, we reminisce about one excursion we took many years ago. These three friends and I are in the same age bracket and at the time of our excursion we were nine or ten; that's more than half a century ago! I don't remember what prompted us to go on this excursion except that kids in those days spent a lot of time playing out in the neighborhood. The four of us huddled and decided to go into town. This was the first time any of us had gone into town without an adult and especially, without permission.

It so happened that all four of us lived on Esquivel Street. The twins, Amador and Manuel Urrabazo, who had come to California with us on that first trip, lived near the end of the street, on the south side. Joe Rodriguez, whom I've mentioned before, lived about halfway between the twin's house and mine, mine being near the north end of Esquivel St.

From Esquivel St. there are three routes to take into town. Gillis, which is only half a block south from where I lived, goes west, and after passing Memo's restaurant, makes a smooth, round turn south. From this point, the name changes to Losoya and eight blocks from this point, is Main St. This is the route we took. Once we were on Losoya, we walked on the east side of the street for a while and then crossed over when we were getting close to the courthouse. This is an historic building that still exists, although it has been remodeled and I understand an unfortunate error was made in the reconstruction, but to this date I do not know what that error is.

As we approached the courthouse, we saw a man sitting and leaning back on one of the large, shade trees close to the sidewalk. As we walked closer to the man, we could see a big gash across his neck; he definitely appeared to be dead! This sight, of course, scared the daylight out of us and we ran off, crossing to the other side of the street as fast as we could! To this day, we question each other as to whether we actually saw this and we all remember that we did. Back on the other side of Losoya, we ran all the way to Main Street, only a few blocks away from the courthouse. Once on Main, we felt safe and turned south onto it and proceeded on our excursion through downtown.

Main Street smelled good, especially when approaching Ross Drug Store or Walgreens. The downtown section of South Main Street we were on, south of Losoya, is not very long; actually, it is no more than three blocks of what I knew as "downtown." Ross drugstore, the very first drugstore in Del Rio, was also towards this end of Main Street, and on the opposite side of the Texas Theatre. A couple of stores down, on the same side of Main, was Walgreens. This was a favorite hangout for upcoming teenagers in the forties and fifties. It had a soda fountain, which was a haven for teenyboppers of the forties. I remember it being Walgreens but it may have been Roach-McMlymont, or Roache's , as everyone called this store; it also had a soda fountain. A most nostalgic memory for those my age was that of the milkshakes and the delicious hamburgers popular with the "healthy" kids of San Felipe.

Here again, I don't remember whether it was Kress's or Walgreens that had two one-foot square pillars outside, in front of the store. The pillars were mirrored on all sides and one of us kids would stand right up to one side and stride an arm and a leg out, around one side. To the amusement of the others, this looked as if we were riding a horse, as they saw two arms and two legs in motion. From sharing this experiences with other, now grown men from Del Rio, I find that as kids, most of them used to perform this little "ritual." There is another silly thing we did on our excursion through town. As we passed by Sears and Roebuck, we would bend down and peek up the women mannequin's dresses. My wife gets a big kick over this whenever I reminisce about this silly thing we kids did; we were too young to know why, but we did it.

Continuing on Main, the next thing I remember of our excursion is walking to Canal St., which, as I mentioned, is towards the end of Main Street with the Texas Theater being near this corner. We walked onto Canal a short distance to where it turns into Cantu, after a long, gradual curve. Now on Cantu, we crossed Canal Bridge, which crosses the San Felipe Creek. Just beyond this bridge, is La Plaza, which has become quite a landmark, all its own. Upon crossing the Canal Bridge, and before reaching La Plaza, we went down to the creek and took our time walking home along the creek bank, just like Tom Sawyer and Huckleberry Finn. We followed the San Felipe Creek, as it sort of parallels Losoya, the street that led us into town, and we knew the creek would eventually lead us back to El Puente Del Martillo. I'm pretty sure this is where we came up onto, where Taini and Johnson meet. From there it's three blocks to Esquivel, at which corner we turned north for a short distance to where the twins lived. Joe and I continued up Esquivel a couple of blocks to Joe's house, from which point I walked the last few blocks to my house. I don't remember at what point our parents confronted us when we got back; I do know that we had lost track of time and it was late afternoon. Since we had left sometime in the morning, we were greeted with great consternation, as by this time our parents had the police looking for us. I don't think anyone of us got spanked; I know I didn't.

Me. Elsa and Locha. (Baby
unknown to me).

Proud sailor boy - maybe five years
old. Sure proud of that uniform!

Four neighborhood friends. Benny Hernandez, Ramiro Ramon, Arnulfo Maldonado and Henry Davis. Right in front of my house (to the left) on Esquivel Street.

Practicing baseball "pick-ups". Esquivel house behind me.

Slingshot Gang. Brother Dofo at right foreground, neighbor brothers on Esquivel Street, Bebe and Boyque Garza (Chale's brothers), me sticking my tongue out, Elsa with hat, and sister Locha. This may be at the time we got in trouble for having the sheep dog chasing sheep on one of the ranches my father worked at.

Dofo in front of Chato's house 1952?

Currie, Dofo and Locha in backyard of Esquivel house.
Tree to left is the one where sister Currie came across a
few scorpions when she went to pick up her bathing suit
off the tree.

Brother-in-law Pablo Salazar (aka Beaver), Richard Perez, me and Teno Flores. Richard lives in San Antonio and Teno took me to visit him before dropping me off at the airport.

Couisin Joe on a visit to his mini-apple ranch in Sabastopol. Cousin Joe died of leukemia a year later; he is one of the best people I have ever known.

A reunion in Del Rio, July, 2006 which I did not attend (I was attending my James Lick reunion a month later). Up front, my best childhood friend, Tony Trevino, Baby is at far end of the table.

Baby (coming home from a date)?

Baby at a popular restaurant in Del Rio where we went to enjoy a glass of ice tea. This photo is from 2003? On one of my visits back home.

CHAPTER 9

SCHOOL DAYS

I was quite surprised to discover that I had flunked the first grade, not once, but twice! I was aware that I had flunked it the first time, but when I looked through my collection of memorabilia, of which my earliest report cards are part, I saw two different years, two different teachers, both regarding the first grade! In addition to this, I had started school late. At the age of seven, while living at the Cortinas address, my mother tried to get me registered in school. We didn't have pre-school or kindergarten then; we went straight to first grade. I think that what happened that first year, was that I was such a problem I was not able to stay in school. My report card for that first year shows a very limited attendance, and that is why I had to repeat first grade the first time. My recollection of that first year was that my poor mother had struggled with me so much getting me to school that alas, I was too much to handle and she relented and took me back home. That was not the case; I was just an ornery kid; indeed, a very poor beginning towards my education. Thus, I started school a year late, couldn't stay the first year, and then officially flunked the second time around. The second time was due to my complete lack of English. My general, average grade was a D with C's and D's in Attitude, Reading and Arithmetic; I just hadn't learned to speak or to write English at this time, although I could understand it a little. In fact, I didn't learn to speak English until I was eight years old. I attribute my poor grades on my lack of English, and perhaps that's why that subject turned out to be one of my favorites.

In the first grade, whenever we had a reading session, I would look over my classmate's shoulder. I tended to panic in fear that I'd be called upon to read. I'd glance over to the desk in front of me and desperately try to find the pictures on the student's book so that I could tell what page we were on; our reader was a Dick and Jane book. In recent years, I have bought four of these nostalgic books at an antique store. One of these, I recently gave as a Christmas gift to my daughter's, then, in-laws, whose names happen to be Dick and Jane. The other three, I am saving, one each, for my three grandchildren.

Fortunately, once I learned to speak English, I turned out to be a better-than-average student throughout my school years, including two years of college. I even made up the year I flunked by skipping fifth grade and being promoted to the sixth. Still, throughout my school years, I was older than most of my fellow classmates.

It was at Cupertino Elementary that I fell in love for the first time; her name was Bonnie, a pretty, cherubic, Japanese girl. This took place in the second grade in 1946. Bonnie was one of the top students in our class and was never aware of my feelings, nor were they reciprocated. Did I mention she was smart? On the other hand, there was this other little girl that followed me around at recess and at lunchtime, everyday. My best friend, Larry Hobbs and I, usually hung out together either out by the swings, each one at our designated swing, with mine being named Trigger; or else we'd be at the baseball field. One day, at lunchtime, Larry and I were finishing our lunch so that we could rush off onto the baseball field when this little girl came by and sat next to me. I was a little irritated and asked her why she was always following us around. She quickly replied, " Because I want to be your girlfriend!" Well, I made a deal with her; I told her that if she played over on the girl's side while I played on the boy's side, she could be my girlfriend. She seemed delighted and she skipped away saying "Okay!" A similar story my son, Robert, recently told me, has to do with my six-year old grandson, Jake. It seems that this little kindergarten classmate of his, professed her feelings for him one day after school. My daughter–in-law, Lori, had gone to pick Jake up and overheard this little girl say, "I like you, Jake! I'm going to marry you!" My grandson, a bit confused, turned to face the little girl and said, "What! You're going to <u>bury</u> me!"

For lunch, I used to take what are now called "burritos," these being a flour tortilla wrapped around scrambled eggs with potato, scrambled eggs with chorizo, or just a plain, bean burrito. I used to be embarrassed about my lunch and would go off with Larry to some isolated spot to eat our lunch; I felt comfortable with Larry. Sometimes I ate in the cafeteria with the rest of the class, but not often. The other students, who took their lunch, usually had a peanut butter and jelly sandwich, neatly cut up in a triangle, and neatly wrapped in wax paper. Along with this, they usually had an apple or some other fruit. These kids took their lunch in a lunch pale; I took mine in a brown paper bag. One of the students, that for years I though was Larry, lived close by, off Highway 9. I went to his house one day to shoot baskets. It was very impressive to me to see a house with a lawn and a sidewalk, not to mention the basketball hoop hanging on the garage. Larry told me, many years later, that it wasn't he, and that he had been as poor as I, and had also picked prunes in the area.

Through the years, I often wondered what had become of Larry or Bonnie or even that little girl that liked me, or any of the other classmates whose names I have long forgotten, but many of whose faces still linger in my mind. One day, about fifty years later, on such a moment of reminisce, I looked up Larry Hobbs in the phonebook. What were the chances that he was still alive? What were the chances that if he were alive, that he would be living in San Jose or even in Santa Clara County, or even in

California? Finding three Hobbs in the phonebook, I called all three and left a message stating that I was looking for an old friend with whom I had gone to school many years ago. I left my phone number, and let it go at that.

The following day I got a call from Larry, amazed and elated as much as I was! He went on to tell me that he remembered me well; he too, had thought of me as his best friend. Amazing as this discovery was, it turned out that Larry lived in the same community as I, about three miles away! A few days later, I met Larry for lunch at a popular Chinese restaurant, here in San Jose. He had the advantage in either one of us recognizing the other; he knew I was Mexican-American. He had advised the waitress, who led me right to where Larry was sitting. The following week, my wife and I had Larry over for dinner, at which time I was brought up to date on my second-grade classmates. He went on through high school with most of them and pointed out that Bonnie had either become a Doctor, or married one. He also gave me a copy of our class picture along with a list of the names of our little classmates. One of the report cards among my memorabilia is from that year, and it shows our teacher to have been Miss Lonnie G. Brewer.

Towards the end of our conversation, I found out that Larry had been the Santa Clara County Tax Collector for several years. Furthermore, he informed me that he was engaged to be married and was planning on moving to Oregon. The last time I spoke with Larry, he was fixing his house up to put it on the market; that was my last contact with this old friend.

I don't remember Miss Brewer except for one incident that involved our weekly "share day." Each Monday, or after a holiday, each one of us was to share what we had done during our time off. My contribution was very bland; it always consisted of going into San Jose with my parents for shopping or to a movie, or working out in the fields. There was one little girl who had the class enthralled with her outings. It seemed that every time, she and her family had gone to Yosemite, Yellowstone, or some other locale that caused interest, along with envy, in the rest of the class. Apparently, Miss Brewer thought it a bit much after a while, and contacted her parents; it had all been made up. The poor girl was confronted in class and made to apologize. I say poor girl because I realize now, that she must have had a need in her life to belong; a need that was realized through "make-believe."

Well, initially, I attribute having done well in my schooling to four childhood classmates, three of them having turned out to be very dear, life-long friends. The first was that cute Japanese girl, Bonnie. The others, all three in Del Rio, were Tony Treviño, Adriana (Nani), and Argentina (Baby) Calderon. While in the second grade, Bonnie had the highest grades, which, along with the grades of my other, three future classmates inspired me to aim at better grades.

I've always considered Tony to be my best childhood friend. He was instrumental in my doing well through the third, fourth, seventh and through the second semester of the eighth grade. Other than my horrific first grade experience, these are the only years I attended school in Del Rio. The first semester of the eighth grade had been at Orchard Elementary, in San Jose, California. Through my schooling in Del Rio, I often did my homework with Tony, and this turned out to be very helpful; especially the section on "diagramming" sentences in our English class; Tony had this down pat. Nani and Baby were also very instrumental in that they too, like Tony, were "A" or "B+" students. I had a crush on Nani in the third and fourth grades, and on Baby in the eighth grade.

For the record, the very first girl I ever had a crush on, was Carmen Arredondo, whose family was a neighbor of my older brother Jose, and his wife, Brijida. In 1943, on a visit to see my newborn nephew, Jose Jr., I saw Carmen for the very first time. As I remember the incident, she was walking across the street. I remember we made eye contact and I was very aware of her looks, even though I was only at the tender age of seven. She was then, and still is, very attractive. Carmen married George Martinez, also from Del Rio and whom I came to know very well here in San Jose. Incidentally, George was a very popular boxer in Del Rio during our childhood. He and Carmen have a beautiful and talented family. For several years George was very active in Del Rio-related functions. On one of these functions, by chance, I ran into him in Del Rio. We were both staying in the same motel without either one of us knowing it. Unfortunately, George passed away very recently.

Nani was the third girl on whom I had a crush, Bonnie, in Cupertino, having been my second "love." My relationship with Nani turned out to be a long-time endearing one, on my part, anyway. First of all, this "relationship" began when she and I were in the third grade. Neither she nor I ever professed any such feelings towards each other; but they were there; I know they were, most definitely on my part. Although, while in high school, and on one of my trips to Del Rio, I had a conversation with a former classmate and very close friend of Nani's. Reminiscing about our grade school years, this friend of hers told me, "Nani has always liked you." And there were signs, through our "courtship," that she, in fact, had feelings for me. My feelings for Nani were always poignant and profound; these feelings were endearing, much like the lyrics from the Man From La Mancha theme song, The Impossible Dream, "to love, pure and chaste from afar."

This pretty person affected me from the very first time I saw her. Although nothing ever came out of this quiet, love-from-a distance, romance, Nani has always held a tight hold on me, and is one of the most memorable, and one of the most admired people in my life. Baby, on the other hand, was my very first "real" girlfriend, this having taken place in the second semester of the eight-grade; she too, as Tony and Nani have, has always been a very deep part of my life. I make it a point to see her every time I visit Del Rio. In the seventh or eighth grade, we had a spelling bee where our very special teacher, Mr. Guardia, pitted the boys against the girls. All the boys lined up against the wall on one side of the room and the girls on the opposite side. The spelling bee went on for a while, and one by one, the students began dropping out. Eventually, it came down to Baby and me; she won, and she still remembers the word; I don't.

All three of these three dear friends of mine carried an "A" or "B+" grade through school, and I mean through most of their school years! Of the four of us, Nani is the only one who went through college. I understand that she went on to become a Speech Therapist in either Eagle Pass or Laredo. Although I lost complete contact with her for over thirty years, I did get to see her at a reunion held in Del Rio a few years ago. It was quite rewarding for me to have seen her once again; it would be quite more rewarding if I were to see her once again.

I owe Tony, Baby and Nani so much; just the friendship alone, is immeasurable. I will forever be grateful to these three friends, as their attention and dedication to school must have rubbed off on me. Each is as much of an institution to me as is the San Felipe Creek, San Felipe High School, and other memorable landmarks, all indelibly imbedded in my heart.

From my school records, I find out that I lived at 412 Urista Street when I was in the seventh grade. This is where my paternal grandmother's house was and apparently, we were renting a place located on this property. It is strange that I don't remember having lived there and certainly not at an age where I should remember. I only have memories of having lived at the Esquivel address through those two years of school.

Tony went to work at Laughlin Air Force Base, which is twelve miles northwest out of Del Rio. This really surprised me, as I imagined him going to college and becoming a teacher or a lawyer. He wound up working for the Army and Air Force Exchange Service for more than 33 years. He retired in 1991 as a GS 15 Area General Manager at the Mid Atlantic Area where he had responsibility for the Military Exchanges in several east-coast states. Now, he is enjoying retirement in San Antonio with his wife, Ella, his childhood sweetheart back in Del Rio. Tony tells me one of his passions is golfing, which he manages to take in at least three days a week. I always knew that if Tony hung around me long enough, he'd amount to something. Alas! The truth of the matter is just the opposite, this as a result of our friendship through those wonderful childhood years.

Tony's son, Tony Jr., is the one who did become a lawyer. He is now a senior partner in a law firm in Laredo, Texas. His daughter, Ella Palmer, is the mother of two children, Ryan, 21 and Michelle, 18, both attending college. His daughter is a Dental hygienist and her husband, Steve, is a director at the State Transportation Division in Austin, where they live. A memory that I shared with Tony recently, is of one day that he and I went fishing. Tony had this small, tin canoe, just big enough for the two of us, and with the San Felipe Creek running right by his property, swimming and fishing were part of our lives. My fishing had always been done with the bamboo rod, and usually, with a pin for a hook. This time, Tony brought out a rod and reel, which was the very first time I had ever used such a contraption. Once we got the canoe in the water, Tony took care of the rowing, while I took care of the fishing. Sitting back to back in the canoe, on my very first cast, I caught Tony's back! Nothing serious, but I know that smarts! Another new contraption I experienced was using the indoor bathroom at Tony's house. I remember him telling me to be sure and put the lid up; now, my wife keeps telling me to be sure and put the lid down!

Baby has always worked in Del Rio, and has always been a very hard worker. She used to work part time at an uncle's medical office while in grade school. Her uncle, Dr. Fermin Calderon, had an elementary school named after him. From the time Baby was seven, she used to help with the dishes at her family's restaurant, "Memos," a local landmark in Del Rio. Up until recent years, Baby had been working as a waitress at this restaurant in the evenings, while, during the day, she worked at a grade school cafeteria; even hip and leg problems didn't deter her from working. She has always been known as "Baby" throughout the community. Besides her relatives, her friends and anyone else that knows her, calls her Baby. She told me recently that the kids at school refer to her as "Miss Baby", "Miss" being a prefix we all used in addressing our teachers, whether they were married or not.

Baby introduced me to one of her sons on one of my visits to Del Rio; boy howdy, I'm close to six feet tall myself, but facing her son, I had to use my peripheral vision to see from one shoulder to the other, while tilting my head up, so that I could see him eye-to-eye! This boy was way over six feet tall. In fact, two Baby's two sons played professional basketball. Recently, her husband passed away and on a more recent visit, Baby informed me that she had cancer. Through all this, she still maintains her strength of character, dignity and lovable personality. She is some kind of woman! Today, December 3, 2007, I received an invitation to Baby's seventieth birthday, to be held at Memo's restaurant on December 16. Unfortunately, I cannot attend, but hope to see her next summer, during the San Felipe High, Exes reunion.

The popular, Memo's Restaurant, was ironically, originally established in 1936, the year I was born. At that time, however, the restaurant was at a different location. The current location is on Gillis Avenue, a beautiful spot along the banks of the San Felipe Creek. Tony used to live directly across Gillis from the restaurant while my other friend, Teno Flores, lives directly across the creek, east of the restaurant. Today, Memo's isn't as popular as before, this partly due to the flood of 1998, during which the restaurant suffered major damages. In fact, the initial source of the flood started just behind the family property. The Calderon family has a street named after them that goes to the back of their property, on which there are three or four family residences. Blondie, Baby's younger brother had several vintage cars that were destroyed, or having incurred severe damage. Tony's house, being directly across the street from the restaurant, was washed away in the flood.

Not long after that horrible experience, the city had a fundraiser and donated a brand new piano to Blondie as a tribute to his contribution to Del Rio and to country music. All of Baby's brothers were talented, self-taught musicians, with Blondie having a successful career. He was known as "Blondie" just as naturally as Baby was known as "Baby." I happened to be in Del Rio a couple of years after the flood, and posed with Blondie by that piano; he was so proud of it. Less than two months after my visit, I got the bad news that Blondie had died of a heart attack. This tragedy occurred on his way to a performance with Ray Price's band. Blondie had been Ray Price's musical arranger for over twenty years. Ray Price, of course, is the legendary, country music star that has been inducted into the Country Music Hall of Fame. All of this has come out of the San Felipe barrio, in my little hometown of Del Rio, Texas. Memo's walls are filled with many of the country-western stars Blondie met throughout his career. Several celebrities have eaten at Memo's. Of note, is Charles Duvall, who used to take some of the cast members of Lonesome Dove to dine there. This mini-series is just one of many productions to take place in and around Del Rio. In Brackettville, which is about 30 miles east of Del Rio, there is a mini-movie set where Lonesome Dove, The Streets of Laredo and many other productions were filmed. John Wayne had a replica of the Alamo built at this location when he filmed his movie, The Alamo. It is still a tourist attraction there, in Brackettville.

Directly east, and one block from Memo's, on the corner of Gillis and Bridge Street, Teno's father owned a foundry. This too, was a well- known "landmark" in Del Rio. Along Bridge Street, Teno's family owned all the houses on the west side of the street, with the exception of the last one, this belonging to the third of my close buddies, Richard Perez, who now lives in San Antonio Of these three dear friends, only Baby and Teno, still live in Del Rio. The entire block of Bridge Street was severely damaged by the flood of 1998. To this day, all but one house has been restored; the house where Teno's mother lived. Beyond that, all along Bridge Street, the other houses incurred severe damage, some, virtually destroyed. Teno has no way to rebuild; the flood damage was far, far too extensive.

That block looks like a tornado tore through it. Teno concentrated his effort and money on the main house, that of his parents. This house was pretty much completely remodeled when he gave me a tour of the inside, a few years after the flood. The house looked a lot larger than how I remembered it when we were kids.

Early grade school photos, probably third and fouth grades.

Larry Hobbs, my buddy in second grade at Cupertino Elementary, 1946. I was to meet up with Larry some fifty years later, here in San Jose.

Backyard BBQ at my house. L. to R.: Tom Dusek, popular former faculty member, Chon Gallegos, all-everything in
football, leading passer in the nation one year at San Jose State
University, (only Jim Plunkett was more prolific in football at
James Lick) me in the middle, Tony Barrera and Eddie Payne,
both very close friends since our freshman year at Lick, (both are
from Del Rio). See my 1936 Radio Flyer behind Eddie?

Skinny Dude, circa 1952
(Freshman at James Lick
High).

Senior pic, 1956
James Lick High School

CHAPTER 10

WEST OF DEL RIO

The hardships we experienced were not as harsh; yet, in many ways, our first trek to California was similar to that of the Joad family in John Steinbeck's novel, The Grapes of Wrath. Our trek west was but one of the thousands of families that headed west during the early forties. Out of necessity they came; they came from many towns, from many states. From Oklahoma, New Mexico, Kansas, and other states, they came. Texas was one of these, and Del Rio was one of the many towns that were affected by that dark, economic cloud. Throughout the country, from the early thirties to the early forties, families were still gripped by the after-effects of The Great Depression. There was no work to be found and unemployment was in the millions. This coupled with the Dust Bowl that engulfed the Great Plains some years earlier, literally forced families to abandon their homes. In Del Rio, the issue was the same, basically lack of work, and this too, put our family in the wake of the mass exodus to California, and other parts west.

In June of 1946, I was aware of the ominous air in our community. More and more there was word of yet another family leaving for California. The week before our first journey, the talk around the neighborhood was about the vast amount of work waiting in the fields and orchards of California. I remember hearing someone say that "money grew on trees" there. To me, that conjured images of just "picking" the money right off the trees! I even asked my mother if I could have a wallet so that I had something to put the money in. I don't remember when my parents finally made the decision to leave Del Rio, nor did I understand the root cause. The move finally came out in the open and the plan to leave Del Rio was put in motion. My mother and father, my sisters Currie and Locha, my brother Dofo and I, were to go on that first journey. I believe my oldest sister, Fane, was already in California, having joined her husband, Santos Elemen, who had gone to California, earlier that year.

I vaguely remember the farewell hugs and kisses of relatives and neighbors as we gathered outside our house on Esquivel. Meanwhile, my father and the man who was the principal driver, did a final inspection on the packing. This is where our trek begins to parallels the Joads family in The Grapes of Wrath. The truck that was to take us to California was overloaded with the belongings of three families. Besides ours, there were two other families, one, consisting of twin, childhood friends, Amador and Manuel Urrabazo, and their mother. The other family consisted of an aunt of the twins, and two of their cousins, Anita and Carlos Barrera. Counting the driver, we totaled thirteen people in that little pickup truck. The pickup had a wood-railed bed that was framed, such as to sustain a canvass top, like a pioneer's covered wagon. Ten of us were crowded in the back, along with the various articles that included some small appliances, clothing and whatever supplies we would need on the road; my mother's Singer sewing machine was among these articles. My father and mother and the driver, sat up front.

As the pickup pulled away, we waved our final good-bys through the opening of the tarp flaps hanging from each side of the pickup. This, we did until we reached the corner of Esquivel and Gillis where we turned right and headed west. It was at this point that I got a saddened pang in the pit of my stomach, a realization that I was leaving my friends, actually going away from Del Rio, somewhere far away, to an unknown place. The pickup was heavily laden with our personal belongings. Hanging outside on the door handles and along the rails of the pickup, were canvas pouches filled with water for the long trip. Tied flat at the rear of the pickup, were the two canvas flaps that closed together in the middle and served as our viewpoint on this fateful journey. Just past Memo's Restaurant, Gillis makes a gradual curve southward, and from this point on, it becomes Losoya. Four blocks down, on Losoya, we turned right again onto what was then Avenue F. This stretch out of Del Rio is really that portion of Highway 90 that eventually leads to El Paso via Interstate Highway 10 from Van Horn. Within a half hour of leaving Esquivel Street, we were out in the open range; an image of Texas popularly held. Sagebrush, mesquite trees and cactus masked the landscape, this and a few rolling hills.

For the next few hours, there was an ominous silence. I'm sure the grownups were feeling the sadness and the hardship of the departure far more than we, the children were. They knew well, the reason for the long, long journey. As for the twins, Amador and Manuel and myself, the journey was an exciting adventure. Once we were out in open land, which seemed to be endless, we spread the rear flaps partly open, just enough to take in the endless open range. The thirteenth person, the driver, was a man whose name I don't remember. I always assumed that he worked for someone in California, to whom he was taking us. I do remember that my father helped with the driving. I am told that there was another man, a fourteenth person on that first trip, but I don't remember anyone else at all; nor can I see how anyone else could possibly have fit in that overloaded pickup.

Langtry was the first town I was to become familiar with on future trips. It's about fifty-five miles from Del Rio. Langtry has a name but consists only of Judge Roy Bean's court/saloon, Museum and a small gift shop, across the street. Other towns I was to become familiar with are Dryden, Sanderson, Marathon, Alpine, Marfa, Van Horn, and a few other dots along highway 90. These little towns were to fill me with excitement as each signaled the closeness to Del Rio on our way back home. Similarly, Las Cruces, Lordsburg and Deming through New Mexico, as well as Benson, Casa Grande, Gila Bend and Yuma through Arizona, these too, became land buoys in our destination to and from California. Like a beacon in the distance, each town lifted my spirits, as each one, in succession, was closer to home. Through all these towns in Texas, and continuing through New Mexico and Arizona, the journey was exciting because the scenery conjured up all the magical fantasies of the westerns we used to watch in the Texas Theater. I was mesmerized by the vastness of the open land and would fall into a daydream of riding a horse at full gallop across this vast, open land. The horse I visualized in my daydreams, was always a palomino horse, most likely because of Roy Rodger's horse, Trigger. How I enjoyed those imaginary adventures!

Whenever we stopped to rest, or because of a flat tire, the twins and I would immediately run out into the open range and seek out "gold" or just pick up rocks to throw about. Occasionally, we'd throw errant rocks at lizards, the like of which are not seen in Del Rio. In Arizona, I was to find out that this lizard was a Gila monster; this is not your ordinary lizard. At some point in time, towards the evening, we would pull off the road and "camp out" for the night. While my father and the driver got a fire going, the women went about preparing dinner. While this was going on, the twins and I would go "exploring." It was like being on a campout, and once again, we'd take off to look for gold and hunt for lizards, snakes or "Indians." When it came time for bed, some of us slept in the pickup, while others slept on the ground, outside with mother earth. On one such occasion, I believe it was in New Mexico, we were awakened, way after mid-night, by the brightness of flashlights. Highway Patrolmen had stopped to check in on us to make sure we were not hurt. One of the officers asked me where my shoes were and I lifted my pillow to show him my shoes, safely tucked away. He laughed and told me that that was a good idea, perhaps because of spiders, scorpions or other desert critters lurking about. It is very likely that my mother told me to put my shoes away, for the reasons stated.

Now and then, during the day, we would pull off the road along an irrigation canal to wash up. On one such occasion, my swimming came into play. I dove underwater and like Johnny Weismueller, I became Tarzan; this was one of the fun parts of the journey. Another one took place along Highway 99, near Bakersfield. Across the highway from where we parked, was a watermelon patch, an amazing sight, as none of us had ever seen one. The twins and I ran across the highway and took a small watermelon each, and thoroughly enjoyed the moment. Flat tires occurred occasionally, and it was interesting to see my father and the driver use a piece of discarded blown-out tire that had been strewn along the highway. This, they called a "boot," which they would insert between the inner tube and the pickup's worn-out tire. Everyone had to get off the truck, which afforded us a nice rest.

Occasionally, we'd pull into a gas station with the radiator boiling over. I don't remember if it was the driver or my father who, this one time, was using a piece of cloth to carefully remove the radiator cap. Invariably, the spewing hot water shot out, causing him to jump back, but not quite fast enough to avoid the hot water. At these gas station stops, the canvass water bags would be filled, and I don't remember how we got fresh water because the tap water we drank at some places through New Mexico and Arizona was salty. Nevertheless, the water bags were filled and again, hung outside the pickup on the door handles or tied to the wooden rails. One item we went for, anxiously, was ice; the heat through Arizona and New Mexico was worse than in Del Rio. Entering California, the weather was still very hot, especially in places like Blythe, Indio and Banning, but once past the Los Angeles area, the heat wasn't bad.

I remember a section of Highway 99 that was lined with eucalyptus trees; I didn't know then, what kind of tree these were, but they are very distinct. One of our rest stops along Highway

99 was under a row of these. There's a little tinge of memory that this may have been the spot where we savored those sweet watermelons.

Between Bakersfield and the152 turnoff, a distance of approximately 150 miles, I remember nothing on that first journey in 1946. Ironically, through this area, including Bakersfield, I was to pick cotton on subsequent returns to California. Approximately 25 miles south of Bakersfield, Interstate Highway 5 and Highway 99 come to a "V", both sides of the "V" going northward. It is between this "V", from Bakersfield to Los Banos, where we picked cotton in several farming communities, these being Shafter, Delano, Corcoran, Mendota, Firebaugh, Tulare and including Bakersfield. I was to attend school in Corcoran as well as in Mendota, in each town, just for the duration of the picking season.

Turning onto Highway 152, my father informed us that our journey was almost over. Not far from the turnoff from Highway 99, is Pacheco Pass, a scenic, but hilly route, with several sharp and dangerous curves. Somewhere after leaving the hilly part of that route, and before we got to Gilroy, we passed a tranquil, wooded area with an open foreground that intermittently exposed a shallow creek snaking in undulating curves towards us for a moment, and than out of sight, and then showing up further down the landscape. This scene made such an impression on me that I always look for it whenever I travel this area; it conjures up a dream of a nice little ranch. Just outside of Gilroy, the valley was vast and green, mostly row crops; a sight that, on that first journey, was also foreign to me. This area is still "country," with several ranches dotting the landscape.

Highway 152 fed us onto Monterrey Road, which goes through downtown Gilroy. At that time, Monterrey Road was a principal route to San Jose; now, Highway 101circumvents downtown Gilroy. San Jose itself is today, surrounded by a multitude of convenient, but ugly, freeways. From Gilroy, it's 30 miles to San Jose, with Morgan Hill in between. Going through Morgan

Hill on Monterrey Road, led us to downtown San Jose, where Monterrey Road comes to a junction with San Carlos Street, in the heart of town and becomes Market Street. At this junction there is a park that in recent years has been renamed Cesar Chaves Park; this park was to become one of those "beacons" for me, signifying journey's end; I was always glad to see this old friend after each long, long journey from Texas.

I recently asked Amador Urrabazo and his aunt, Anita, if they remembered where their family had been dropped off upon our first arrival in San Jose. They remember it to have been at a little farming community that lies between San Jose and Milpitas, called Berryessa. Here, in subsequent years, I was to pick apricots and cherries during the summers. Of our own destination, I remember seeing oceans of green vegetation, these being fields of carrots. Also, and very prominent, I remember the hangers at Moffet Field, two giant buildings overpowering the landscape. Because of these hangers, I thought we were in the Alviso area, which is adjacent to Sunnyvale where the hangers are; but in fact, we were either in Monte Vista or in Cupertino, that first year.

There is a cloudy, murky recollection concerning my stay in Monte Vista and in Cupertino. I have memories of having lived at both of these places, but I can't remember for sure, which one we lived at first. Because I have more nostalgic memories concerning Cupertino, I can only assume that we lived in Monte Vista a short while, and most of the year in Cupertino. Monte Vista was, and still is, a very small town. The house we lived in may have belonged to relatives or close friends from Del Rio.

This house was just a few blocks from Stevens Creek Blvd., a main street between San Jose and Cupertino. Stevens Creek Blvd. becomes San Carlos Street in San Jose. While living in Monte Vista, I remember walking to "town" to buy candy, bubble gum or a soda, at the local grocery store. I walked along the railroad tracks, which paralleled our street. I enjoyed walking along the tracks, trying to stay on them as long as possible, just as I used to do in Del Rio. One thing I didn't do in Monte Vista, was to place a nail or a penny on the tracks to have a train run over them. I think that most boys, in most any small town that had a railroad passing through it, did this. I did, in Del Rio. The penny, of course, would be flattened, into an elongated shape. The nail, however, was flattened into a piece of art. Placing the nail in line with the track, the nail would invariably be flattened into the shape of a sword!

Across the street from the house, and not more than two blocks over, there was, what I think now, a packinghouse. This place had a loading ramp that was a little high for me to jump onto. Another boy my age, and who also lived in the same house with us, and I, would jump up on it up to our bellies and then pull ourselves up the rest of the way, proudly walking about it, surveying our surroundings. This was no San Felipe Creek adventure, but we got a kick out of being able to climb this ramp. This boy and I became good friends through our duration in Monte Vista, although, his name escapes me and I have since lost track of him. There was a curiosity about him in that, every time he said anything, he repeated it, verbatim, in a whisper. I finally asked him about this, and he told me that he didn't know why, and that most of the time he was actually not aware of it.

In 1973, and into 1981, I worked as a System Designer for Measurex Corporation, a "batch" process equipment manufacturer for the paper and pulp industry. It just happened that Measurex was located on Bubb Road in Cupertino, just a couple of blocks over from street I had lived on in Monte Vista. One day, my boss asked me to go with him to a warehouse where we kept our equipment. It had been raining for a while, and word came from the warehouse that some of the units might have gotten wet. My boss drove, and heading out of the parking lot, he turned up towards Stevens Creek Blvd., onto which he turned left, towards Monte Vista. It was at this point that I felt the nostalgia of having lived in Monte Vista. The nostalgia got immensely stronger as my boss turned onto the street I had lived! As we drove closer to where I remembered the house to have been, I saw the ramp! It now looked like what it was, a small, loading ramp that now, I could jump onto with ease, which my boss and I did. This place, that more than thirty years before I thought was a packinghouse, was now our warehouse! My boss and I went in and the thought of when I used to play around this old friend ran through my mind; I had been curious then, as to what was inside.

Cupertino, which is less than 5 miles from Monte Vista, holds more memories for me, as this is where we lived while I attended second grade at Cupertino Elementary. The school was located on the corner of Stevens Creek Blvd. and Saratoga-Sunnyvale Rd., now known as DeAnza Blvd.; at the time it was actually a two-lane road between Sunnyvale and Saratoga known simply, as Highway 9.

Our dwelling during this period in Cupertino was a large, weathered, two-story barn house that was centrally located within a prune orchard. From Stevens Creek Blvd., it was approximately two miles west, towards Saratoga. At any given time, while we lived there, at least three other families lived in this old barn house, as well. The other families were relatives or acquaintances from Del Rio. My two oldest brothers, each, with his own little family, lived with us for a short time. A niece of my mother's, Felipa Carabajal, the cousin whom I always thought of as my aunt, also lived there at one time, along with her husband Juan and their five daughters. It is interesting enough that this family consisted of only girls, but the names of these five girls are more interesting, in that each name starts with an "O" and ends with an "A." Chronologically, they are: Olivia, Odelia, Oralia, Ofelia and Odilia.

While living in Cupertino, picking prunes was what most of us did. We didn't have far to go to work; the orchard was all around us. Picking prunes was arduous work, being on our knees most of the time, which made for long days. Each of us, with our own buckets, would pick the prunes as fast as possible; we were paid by the number of boxes filled. The boxes, or, crates into which we emptied each bucket, were neatly stacked along paths within the orchard. These boxes, which were used in picking various crops, were to serve us as furniture, at a later time.

I'm pretty sure that my mother and father were working at a cannery in San Jose at this time, while the rest of the family picked prunes. I remember this because my mother would usually bring me a Baby Ruth or a Hershey's candy bar every evening after work. My sister, Currie, tells me that she and Millie, a teenage girl her age, were attending Fremont High at the time, and that during summer, they worked cutting apricots, nearby, in Cupertino.

Millie's parents were one of the families that lived at the barn house. She was the oldest of three siblings, the other two being two brothers, one named Alex, who was my age, and the other named Leo. During our free time, Alex and I would wander around the orchard looking for rabbits, playing cowboys or just wandering about. Many days, I spent alone, and I remember at these times carrying my Gene Autry holster set with the cap pistol loaded; no creature was safe. I sure wish that I had kept that holster set; I've seen the prices of such toys at antique shops, recently.

I believe the chapter, "The Scent of The Seasons," was triggered here, in Cupertino one early autumn during one of my wanderings about the orchard. I vividly remember walking alone one late afternoon, some distance from the barn house, on the west side of the orchard. I was walking towards a canal that bordered the orchard, and looking up at the sky, which was grayish for the most part, with patches of blue scattered about. It wasn't cold; the sun shown through the grayish clouds, but I could feel the coolness of autumn. The patches of gloom in the sky, with the sun still dominating, made something in me sense a "scent" of the season. I experienced a similar feeling while in my mother's backyard in San Jose, this, while in high school. Since then, I get this "scent' of the seasons every year.

Cupertino, in 1946, was mostly fruit orchards, with few

businesses. My parents did their weekly shopping in San Jose, during which time I usually went to a movie. For other family recreational outings, we would go to Stevens Creek Park on weekends, the park being just above Monte Vista. This park offered picnic grounds and a scenic tour, but principally, what attracted us to this place was the large reservoir. It was a gathering place where people would sit at the top and enjoy watching water skiers and maybe some swimmers; over this, there was usually a fisherman or two, on the far side bank.

On one such outing, my nephew, Jose Jr., who is 7 years younger than I, got too close to the edge of the reservoir embankment and rolled down into the water. My brother, Dofo and others, ran after him and got him out before any damage was done. During a workday, while we were in the fields, this time picking carrots, this same nephew, whom we called "Papi," came upon an unusually large and weird-shaped carrot. It was about the size of a five-pound bag of sugar and oblong in shape. I tried to pick it up only to have it fall on my foot. We took this unique carrot home and for some reason, I claimed it as mine; this is the only memory I have of us having picked carrots.

For the better part of that first year, while living in Cupertino, two brothers from Mexico were living with us. My mother, bless her heart, basically "adopted" these boys; she washed their clothes, fed them and scolded them, just as she did any one of us. These two brothers became an extension of our family, staying in touch with the family for many years thereafter. These two brothers, Juan and Arturo Terrazas, were very charismatic and of good character. One of them played the guitar and the two would usually serenade the girls on their birthdays.

We lost track of Arturo, but about ten years ago, on a visit to Del Rio with my high school buddy, Eddie Payne, I made it a point to visit Juan in Eagle Pass, which is 55 miles east of Del Rio. My sister Currie, who had kept in touch with him through the years, had given me his address and suggested I look him up. I had no idea how to find Juan in Eagle Pass, as I had never been to this border town. It just happened that we were also visiting a friend of Eddie's across the border, in Piedras Negras and his friend's wife, who worked in Eagle Pass, came to pick us up. She happened to be familiar with Eagle Pass, and very shortly found the street and the house I was looking for. I got to visit Juan briefly, as we recalled our life in Cupertino. He broke into tears when I informed him that my mother had passed away. Sobbing, he said, "She was like a mother to me." A few years later, I got to see him once more, for the last time; Juan passed away just months after that last visit.

At the corner of Stevens Creek Blvd. and Highway 9, there were two landmarks that I still hold in this nostalgic pocket of my mind. One of these is the Cali Brother's Feed and Grain store with two silos off to the side, reaching skyward. The other, directly across from the Feed and Grain store on Stevens Creek Blvd., was a general store that I want to believe was a "Red & White" general store. We used to shop there for work clothes and other supplies, such as kneepads for picking prunes.

For some reason, the rolls of BB chain they had on display were of particular interest to me. This chain can be see in bank and motel counters, used there to keep their pens from walking away. I'd ask my mother to buy me a certain length of this chain with which I learned a little "roping " trick. Holding one end of the chain between my thumb and middle finger of my left hand, while pointing my first finger straight out, I'd throw the chain towards that finger, with my right hand, simultaneously twisting the chain to create a loop. My goal was to have that loop travel through the length of the chain and "rope" my extended finger. Another thing I did with the chain, that I'm sure many kids did, was to wave it back and forth on a flat surface and watch it "snake" itself along the surface; I still do that today whenever I'm at a bank, (patiently) waiting for my transaction to be processed.

A humorous, disappointing, and even more so, embarrassing to my father, was an incident that occurred while living in the barn house. It was either a fellow co-worker of my father's or a drinking buddy he met at a local bar who "sold" him a small trailer house. This mobile trailer was parked in the middle of a prune orchard across Highway 9, not far from the barn house. One evening, my father, very excitedly, drove us to see the trailer house he had "bought." We were impressed; it was very clean and "homey." My father gave us the grand tour while informing us how he came across this purchase for only $100 dollars. Unfortunately, it turned out to be a scam, and although we were all able to laugh about this, after the disappointment, I've always felt bad for my father; he felt so proud thinking he had done a good thing for his family, only to find out he had been taken.

After school was over, we stayed through the summer working in the fields, after which we went back to Del Rio. The journey back was a little easier, as we had our own transportation now, and we were a little more comfortable. It was still an arduous trip, though, and it took us several days to complete. But the buoys, those little town beacons that guided us closer and closer to home, seemed quite friendlier on the way back. I stayed in Del Rio through the school years 1947 through 1949. I don't remember going back to California during the summer months of those two years. At this time, I attended School Number2, this school better known as "La Escuela Calavera." I think that it is safe to assume that this school was called such, because of its proximity to the cemetery; "Calavera" means skull.

For Christmas, in 1947, I got my first bicycle, which I like to think was a Shwinn, but I really don't remember that, it in fact, it was. I do remember it had all the features of a Shwinn, with the tear- drop head light on the front fender, and the body that was also tear-shaped with the horn on the side. On the back, it had a rack on which I tied my books; and of course, it had the wide, white sidewall tires. I especially appreciated the shock-spring along the front, just below the handlebars; the streets in my neighborhood were very bumpy.

I also remember catching my mother and father coming

out of Montgomery Ward with the bicycle. They were just as surprised to see me, as the bicycle was supposed to be my Christmas present. My friend and next-door neighbor, Chale and I, just happened to be on one of our childhood jaunts downtown. My parents, a little disappointed, let me take the bicycle home, which I walked because I didn't know how to ride it well enough to take any chances. I seem to recall the bicycle being a deep red in color.

It was during this period, through the third and the fourth grade that I came to know those life-long friends, Tony Treviño, Teno Flores and Richard Perez. It was also during this time that I met Adriana (Nani). Every recess or lunchtime, Nani and I were usually together, this through the third and fourth grades. This sweet, innocent and most poignant romance went on long after I had made California my home

Through this period of time, I have retained memories of some experiences that took place in Corcoran and in Mendota, but have lost track of the actual timing. I know I attended third and fourth grades in Del Rio, yet, I also know that I attended school, for some time, in both Corcoran and Mendota. Certainly, being a migrant farm working family explains my going back and forth, not only between Del Rio and California, but also between many places within California, following the seasonal crops. I attended no less than five different grade schools in California. Therefore, the only thing I can conclude, concerning the period between the third and the fourth grades, is that I attended at least one quarter of each grade in Mendota and Corcoran, respectively, and finished both grades in Del Rio.

In Mendota, we lived in what can well be described as a "shanty town." It was a migrant farm working camp, surrounded by a grove of eucalyptus trees on one side, and a rat-infested, irrigation canal on the other side. There was a "recreational" center that had a jukebox and plenty of dancing area. The mambo was just getting popular than, and I remember trying it, much to the amusement of my brother, Dofo. I was certainly not then, nor have I ever been, a good dancer. For fun, a group of kids my age and I would hunt down rats, which as I stated, were in abundance. One evening, we were chasing some rats in an open area between the cabins and they led us to a small, fallen tree. A couple of the bigger kids moved the tree aside while the rest of us were at the ready with our BB guns. The sight made the toughest of us cringe; there seemed to be hundreds of rats under the main branch. They came in all sizes, some very large, some very young, ugly and pinkish in color. The rats scattered in a fan-like pattern, all heading for the canal as we shot as many as we could, but the number of rats was so great, the majority got away.

Another experience I recall is of a time we went out a distance from the camp into the grove of eucalyptus trees, these, again, in neat row. Seeing this, one of us got the idea of climbing one tree to see how far we could go from tree to tree without having to come down. From my "Tarzan" days in Del Rio, I was able to gather the incentive and confidence to accept the challenge, along with most in the group; the oldest in the group and I, were the ones who went the farthest. On the way back to our camp, the oldest kid in the group was ahead of me and the neatly, rolled up comic strip in his rear pocket caught my attention. With all of us wearing jeans, I got the idea to shoot at this guy's rear pocket, as I knew it would not hurt. I was kind enough to ask him first, to which he replied, "You do and I'll shoot you with my rifle." While the rest of us kids had a BB gun, this older kid had a twenty-two-caliber rifle; I didn't believe he would actually shoot at me, besides, I was so sure that I would hit my target without hurting him.

Taking aim at his rear pocket, I pulled the trigger. His reaction was quick; he turned around and fired the rifle in my direction. I don't know just how close the bullet got to my left ear, but I think I heard it go by, very close! We all continued on our way back home as if nothing had happened and I didn't let him know that he had scared me, nor that I couldn't hear out of my left ear

113

for a few minutes.

While in Mendota, I attended school for the first quarter, I believe. This is where I can't correlate the time between Mendota and Corcoran, where I also attended school for a while. An interesting occurrence took place while attending school in Mendota. One of the kids that lived at the same camp was also in my class. His name was Steve Pargas, who was also to be a classmate of mine in the eighth grade, while at Orchard Elementary, in San Jose.

This one day, a girl whom I liked (and I think, also liked me) was standing right in front of me, talking to the teacher. She was wearing jeans and just happened to have a "well-rounded" personality. Well, the temptation was too great for me and I turned around to get Steve's attention, directing it the girl's bottom. Believe it or not, I then proceeded to poke her with my pencil! Of course the poor girl yelled out in pain. The teacher, a male, put his hands on her shoulders, moving her aside. Facing me, stern look on his face, he asked, "What did you do?" Flabbergasted, I was at a loss for words. Immediately, the girl stepped in and said, "He didn't do anything. I backed up into his pencil." She had to have liked me! I can't believe I did that, and if I should ever meet up with that girl again, I will apologize, most emphatically.

The next thing I remember of this school period, took place in Corcoran. Here again, we were living in a migrant farm working camp, only this time, instead of "shanty" cabins, we were living in tents. The "super" or head contractor of the camp, was the father of a childhood friend and neighbor of mine on Esquivel Street, in Del Rio. This was the Ramirez family and the boy's name is Carlos. In Del Rio, Carlos lived on the corner of Esquivel and Gillis, the corner where Gordo, my dog, bit a man. The Ramirez family is a very good-looking family, including the boys. They all have "smiling" eyes and dimples, and good dispositions, along with great personalities. The second to the youngest, Elvira (Vera) is especially beautiful. I think I had a crush on her even before we started school; we grew up fast, in Del Rio.

Now, in Corcoran, we were a little older and Vera was now, even prettier. She, Carlos and I went to school while living in this tent city. On some days, after school, Vera would tend a "make-shift" store that her father managed for the camp residents. On those days, I would go there on the pretence of buying something. I would tease her by pointing to an item and as she went to get the item, I would say 'No, how about that one over there." I'd do this two or three times at which time she would laugh and I, of course, would then, buy something. Many years later, in San Jose, we happened to meet at a dance and while we were dancing, I mentioned those times in Corcoran and asked if she remembered, to which she replied, "No, I don't remember." Oh well, that's not the only time I've had my bubble burst.

While living in Del Rio, Carlos and I used to play cowboys around his house. One day, we dug up a trench, poured water in it and then filled it up with dirt. On top of this, we put a piece of cardboard on which we sprinkled a layer of dirt for disguise. We then went and recruited other kids to come join in our game. We'd have them chase us around the yard a few times and then lead them to the "booby trap" over which we would jump, and into which they would fall, ankle deep in mud.

In Corcoran, one morning on our way to school, Carlos and I saw a football lying on the sidewalk in front of a house just a few blocks from the tent city. Neither one of us said anything, but our thoughts were the same. On our way back home, the football was still there. I told Carlos to run for a pass as I quickly picked up the football and threw it to him. Immediately, I ran as fast as I could past Carlos, and he then threw the football to me. Thus, we continued all the way home, and to this day, I don't remember who wound up with the football.

One late evening, we were playing hide and seek with several of the kids in the camp. The tents were lined up in a certain way that included bracing of two by fours in-between every other tent. At one point of the game, we were all running as fast as we could to go hide. By this time, it had gotten dark and Carlos ran right into one of the two by fours. It didn't knock him out, but he got thrown to the ground hard and the blow tore off a mole that he had near one ear.

After the fourth grade, we came back to California, not knowing that I was not to live in Del Rio again; that is, not on a permanent basis, as I did attend the seventh grade all year, and as I mentioned, the second semester of the eighth grade. In subsequent years, we did come back to Del Rio, but only for the Christmas holidays. On none of these subsequent trips, did we stay in motels; we drove straight through, as they say, with rest stops as needed. All our trips took two to three days, with the exception of our very first trip in that overloaded pickup; that first trip took us at least four days.

On the way back to California, from one of our later trips and somewhere well out of Del Rio, I took over and drove while my father got some well-earned sleep. After I had been driving for a few hours, everyone had fallen asleep. I kept myself amused with the many rabbits I kept seeing along the road. Pretty soon, there were rabbits that started running across the two-lane highway. There were so many rabbits that I couldn't avoid running over some of them. I felt the car bouncing up and down as if I was going across a series of railroad tracks. The car started to slow down as if I was driving in sand, eventually coming to an abrupt halt. That woke me up! I had fallen asleep at the wheel and was dreaming all this time; the car was riding on sand, because I had crossed over to the other lane and onto the far side shoulder! Needless to say, everybody woke up and my father took over again. I find it hard to believe that another vehicle was not coming towards us at that time, nor that I didn't crash into a telephone pole; my merciful co-pilot was with me on that day, as He has, throughout my life.

On that final trip from Del Rio, in 1949, we wound up living approximately twelve miles south of Bakersfield, and approximately five miles east from Highway 99. We lived in a rural area some miles east of Greenfield, but I don't remember the exact location. I do see on the California map, East Side Canal being near the town of Lamont, and I certainly remember a canal right along one side of the property on which we lived. Perhaps it was Lamont by where we lived, although I've always thought it to be Arvin, which is also in the same vicinity, and also close to that canal I remember.

While attending school at Greenfield Union Elementary, we lived with my grandmother, "Mama" Faustina and her second husband, Francisco Lomas, on a large plot of land. This plot of land was mostly open range, except for the main house and a little "foreman's" quarters some two hundred yards from the main house. My grandmother, her husband and my cousin, Rolando, lived in the main house while we lived in the smaller quarters; we, being my mother and father, my sister, Locha and my brother, Dofo, and of course, the kid from Del Rio.

The land on which we lived was at an intersection where, three plots across the road were agricultural. Kitty corner from our side, in the direction of Greenfield, the land was an ocean of alfalfa. Surrounded by this lush, green carpet, was a house where a family from Oklahoma lived. I used to go visit a boy there that went to school with my cousin and I. I really enjoyed the walk across this alfalfa carpet, running through it part of the way and rolling on it a few times. On one such visit, my friend was feeding pieces of an apple to their horse. Just as I got there, I got to see him get bitten by the horse. It had just chomped down on all four of my friend's fingers. Fortunately, the horse let go right away, but the tops and bottoms of all four fingers had an in-line dent that was very noticeable and I'm sure, very painful. My friend didn't cry, although his eyes did tear.

Parallel to one of the crossroads, north to south and adjacent to the property we lived on, was an irrigation canal. I believe it could have been East Side Canal, which I see in the California map. This canal was a haven for my cousin and me, as we swam

117

and fished there. We also shot frogs with our BB guns. In an earlier chapter, I mentioned an incredible fish story of mine, back in Del Rio. Well, here at this canal, one day I was playing "Tarzan." I had a spear I had made out of a wooden pole, with one end whittled to a point. Standing on the overpass of the canal, I saw a fish directly below me and threw my spear at it. I didn't spear the fish, but I actually hit it, which was pure chance, as anyone knows, because of the refraction properties. The fish isn't where one sees it, because the line of vision is bent between the water surface, and where the fish really is. Anyway, I was a kid, I didn't know about refraction, and I didn't let out a Tarzan cry; I just claimed my prize.

The small house where my family lived was on the far side of the property from the canal. Just beyond this house, the open range began, and this is where we had the most fun. One day, my brother Dofo, cousin Rolando and I, went out "exploring". As we walked by a tree stump, my brother thought to look inside it and found a baby cottontail rabbit. We took it home where my brother and I made a wire cage for it, only to find it gone the following morning. How it got out is still a mystery to me. On another outing, Rolando and I turned over a large piece of plywood. Under it, were several weird-looking bugs, but what caught our attention was a tiny snake not much bigger than an earthworm. Once again, we took it home and later on, in the evening, a full-size snake was crawling in front of our house. My mother told me that it was looking for its baby and that we should put it back from where we had taken it. This, I did, pronto!

My cousin Rolando had a twenty-two rifle, with which we used to hunt rabbits. Just around the corner from our house, in the same general area where we had up-righted the sheet of plywood, a bunch of rabbits congregated, but quickly disappeared upon our arrival. This one time, I went over to the main house and asked Rolando if he wanted to go hunting. He said he didn't have any shells and I only had one left, so we flipped a coin to see who would take the rifle; I won the toss.

Walking back past my house, I turned the corner and sure enough, a bevy of rabbits ran off. Just in front of this clearing, there was an old, dilapidated, corral fence. I went over to it and sat inside, with the rifle at the ready. Soon the rabbits began to return, one by one and as soon as there were several to choose from, I aimed the rifle at a particular one. I aimed at the middle of the rabbit's body in case I was off in any direction. I fired, and saw the rabbit go down. Surprised, startled or whatever, I stood frozen, looking at the rabbit. Then, it took off into the thicket and I ran after it, but to no avail; I couldn't find it. Sadly and very disappointed, I walked over to my cousin's house and told him my sad story.

Walking back to my house from my grandmother's, I felt I just had to go back and look for the rabbit; I knew I had hit it. I went over to the spot where the rabbit had gone down and started looking all around. Then I heard a ruffle in one of the bushes and when I looked inside, the rabbit was in its death throws. Had I waited a little longer, or given up altogether, I would not have found it on time. That evening, my mother prepared a very nice dinner for me.

The most fun Rolando and I had that year, was at school. The school year was 1949-1950 and we were both in the fifth grade, although, a few weeks into the fifth grade, I was promoted to the sixth grade. Our teacher in the fifth grade was Miss A. Naney, whereas, my sixth grade teacher was Miss Button. I dreaded going into a different class and leaving my cousin and my other classmates. I told Miss Naney I didn't want to go into the sixth grade and of course, she said it was best for me. Actually, I was also a little scared about going into a higher grade. In retrospect, this promotion made up for one of the years I had flunked the first grade.

While at Greenfield Elementary, Rolando and I were in the drama class through which we got our claim to fame in the arts by being cast in the play, Snow White And The Seven Dwarfs. Rolando played the part of Bashful, and I played the part of the

Prince. The show was a big hit with the PTA as well as with all the students. As a reward, the entire cast was taken to see the professional play in downtown Bakersfield.

Among our peers, Rolando and I were good at softball, which we played often during recess or at lunchtime. We hit so many homeruns each, that the kids started keeping count. Somehow, the word got out and one day, an older kid approached us on trying out for their team; he was a member of a baseball team that played hardball, not softball, as we did. One Saturday, we went to a city park for our "tryout." All the kids were older than we were; they may have been eighth graders. We were allowed a certain number of "ups" to check our hitting. We each struck out three times in a row, but the one time we did hit the ball, each one of us hit it over the fielder's head; that was the bittersweet end to our baseball career.

Basically, while on this stay in Bakersfield, we were picking cotton. It's amazing to me now, how we endured the daily ritual. Around five- thirty in the morning, with the weather bitter cold outside, my father would wake us up to get ready for the fields. We'd have breakfast and a cup of coffee while huddling around a large barrel, where a nice warm fire was burning. Taken to the fields in Rolando's grandfather's truck, we drove the twelve miles as daylight was breaking. Usually, we'd be at the cotton fields by seven, but because of the dew making the cotton heavier, and since we were paid by weight, the contractor had us wait until the cotton was dry enough to be picked. Meanwhile, we huddled around that old stand-by furnace: the fifty-gallon barrel.

Once we got the word to start, we'd start at one end of a row and the wagon, in which we dropped the cotton, got farther and farther behind us as we worked our way away from the front of the field. Stooping over with the cotton sack strapped across our shoulder, we'd reach out with both hands, rapidly, on either side of the row, plucking the cotton balls from their hard, five-point, sharp-prong "cradles." Many pairs of cotton gloves were shredded during the week. We would continue this laborious, backbreaking work until the sack was tightly packed full. Stooping thusly, and with the sack getting heavier, I marvel that my angel mother was there, right along with my father and her siblings. Each sack was filled as tightly as possible, as we were paid by the weight.

The trick to filling the sack tightly was to periodically stand the sack up and slam it down on its rear. As the sack got too full to lift up and down, we would sit down and while holding on to the open mouth of the sack with both hands, we'd push the cotton in with our feet. The length of the sacks varied, with the stronger men pulling a sack that was eight to ten feet long. Once the sack was full, we had to, somehow, reach just beyond its middle and swing it over our shoulder; thus, we carried it to the trailer, with each sack carried farther and farther away. Pulling the longer sacks over one's shoulder was difficult, sometimes requiring assistance from a co-worker.

Once the sack was balanced over the shoulder, it was carried to the trailer to be weighed after which, the sack was lifted over the shoulder and carried up a ladder onto a ramp that lay across the trailer, from side to side. Here, the back of the sack was opened and while still holding it over one's shoulder, with an up and down motion of the legs, the cotton would be loosened and emptied from both ends of the sack into the trailer. I was too young to carry a real sack, so I either had a small custom sack, or a very short one. It was exciting each time I had my fully-packed "sack' weighed. Since we got paid in cash at each weigh-in, at the end of the day, I would have a few dollars in my pockets! The adventure of climbing up onto the ramp and emptying the sack, added to the excitement.

This "excitement" was carried out in Mendota, Corcoran and in a couple of other agricultural towns scattered about Kern County and Fresno County. One exception was a season that we spent in Casa Grande, Arizona. What I remember of this time is that we lived in adobe cabins that were attached, forming rows of these dwellings. I remember the heat and getting to seeing many Gila monsters up close. Unfortunately, I don't remember the actual experience of being out in the cotton fields during this time, nor do I remember which year we were there.

The most impressive experience on this stay was my seeing real live Native Americans. These First Americans, as I call them, are of great interest to me; somehow, I can identify with their way of life. Many of our most famous frontiersmen lived with one tribe or another and learned their respective language. Kit Carson, among others, married Native American women and many of these men stated that they preferred the Indian's way of life to that of the white's. Each time we went into downtown Casa Grande, it was common to see these "people of the earth" walking about town, or gathered at a corner with other Native Americans. These were Navaho Indians, but to me, they looked like Mexican-Americans. In fact, as we walked by one group, I was expecting to hear them speaking Spanish.

From the cotton fields of Kern, Kings, Fresno and Madera counties, and from all those towns that, each, has left a short, blinking glow of memories, these towns being Bakersfield, Shafter, Corcoran, Tulare, Mendota, Firebaugh and Dos Palos, from all of these places, we always went back to San Jose, and eventually made it our home. All of these migratory, farm-working excursions of which I write, took place between the years of 1946 and 1950. Memories of some of the events I experienced at any one of these places, are well cradled in the warm clasp of the hippocampus sector of my mind; the memories of the timetable, as to when or where these memories took place, are also there, but scattered about its chambers.

Back in San Jose, we were still migrant farm workers in that we were still picking various crops grown throughout Santa Clara Valley. In fact, besides picking cotton in the early years, later on, in the fields of Santa Clara County, we picked prunes, apricots, carrots, tomatoes, cherries, pears and walnuts. Picking walnuts has always been my favorite, because they are larger and lighter than prunes or apricots; therefore, I could fill buckets a lot faster and carry them to the waiting boxes with less strain. Picking tomatoes was also a favorite, simply because I like tomatoes a lot and there were a lot to be eaten. Along with our typical "burrito" lunch, we would always take salt and pepper along with chile peppers. Them tomatoes tasted mighty fine!

On this final trek to San Jose, the first two residences we lived in involved living in a tent. One was on Dale Avenue, which crosses Alum Rock Avenue, north and south, Alum Rock Ave. being a main artery through east San Jose. I remember the Carabajal family, with the five daughters, also living at this place, and also living in a tent. Both tents were in the backyard, and it turns out that the Jimenez family owned this house on Dale Ave., the same family that owned the house on Cortinas Street, where we lived when I was born. The youngest boy from this family, Tony, went to James Lick High, with me, although we didn't pal around very much. It was very common, in the forties and early fifties, to have relatives or friends from Del Rio put up others for a while; such was the case with the Jimenez family.

The memory I have of having lived on Dale Avenue has to do with the lunches my mother used to pack for us. She would make several, of what we call today, "burritos," each a mouthwatering delight. Some would be made with chorizo and eggs, others with potato and eggs, and some, just beans. Whichever she chose to make, these she rolled up in her homemade tortillas. How I looked forward to lunchtime!

While on Dale Ave., I remember picking apricots somewhere in Santa Clara, which is about twenty miles from Dale Ave. For some reason, I remember going home from an apricot orchard that was near El Camino Real and the two youngest Carabajal cousins, Ofelia and Odelia, were either with us, or behind us, in their parent's vehicle. What I also remember is that I had reached an age that would cause me embarrassment if I were seen working in the fields, especially by girls. Many orchards bordered right up to residential areas and often, when we were picking close to someone's house, I could hear kids playing in their yards and I would dread being seen picking apricots, or whatever crop we were picking.

The second place I remember having lived in a tent was on Jackson Avenue, which also crosses Alum Rock Avenue north and south, and is four or five miles west from Dale Avenue. This time, the tent was in the middle of a prune orchard that went east from Jackson Ave. to Capitol Avenue. There were other families living in this orchard, with one other family, also living in a tent. There was an old farmhouse in which one of the families lived. I don't remember who these other families were, but there were a couple of boys with whom I hung around.

Through the orchard, between Jackson and Capitol Ave., there was a clear path that we used to take when going to a fruit stand directly across the orchard on Capitol Ave. Along this path, there were several bee hives spread out throughout a tomato patch. One day, on our way back from the fruit stand, my friends and I decided to throw rocks, or dirt clots, at the beehives. This was not a smart thing to do, as we found out; we were suddenly surrounded by swarm of bees! We ran down the path as fast as we could, getting stung all the while. Screaming and hollering, the three of us ran home along the path and for some reason, I decided to hit the ground, perhaps just to hide within the tomato plants. While lying on the ground, the coolness of the tomatoes seemed like a good thing for easing the pain. I grabbed tomato after tomato and desperately squashed each one all over my face and neck. This did seem to ease the pain somewhat, so I got up and walked the rest of the way home, still a little frightened. The next day, the other boys had ugly swelling about their faces and necks; one had an eye almost shut. Surprisingly, I didn't have any swelling at all! I can only attribute this to the acid in the tomatoes, but I don't know that to be a fact.

In September of 1951, we moved to Bonita Avenue in northeast San Jose, of which I don't have many recollections. I do remember that we didn't live in a tent at this time, and that we only lived at this location for less than two months. One memory

I do have while living on Bonita, is my brother Dofo's mid-forties Buick; we had to push it every morning to get it started. This was a daily ritual before my brother dropped me off at school on his way to work. At this time I was in the eighth grade attending Orchard Elementary, which at that time, fronted Gish Road, with Old Oakland Road cornering the east side. The address was 711 E. Gish Road. This school is now located farther north, towards Milpitas, still on Old Oakland Road. The school is now a beautiful state-of-the-art school with an equally state-of-the-art campus. Orchard Elementary was to be the defining moment that was to take me from the migratory pattern that had started out of Del Rio and through many towns and many schools throughout California. At the time I was attending Orchard Elementary, I had gone to seven different grade schools.

Locha, Currie, family friend and me: probably in Arizona.

On the way to the fields. Me, (don't remember name of kid behind me), Locha in background and Currie on right.

The Kid picking prunes in Cupertino (late forties).

Currie and family friend, top row: cousin Odelia Carbajal and Currie's long-time friend, Millie Turrubiate.

Sister-in-law, Brigida Rincon Lara.

Brother Jose with son Robert (Beto) on his lap, Locha holding niece Berta, Brijida (Jose's wife) and the Kid, drinking coffee.

Me and my "whispering" friend in Monte Vista. 1947.

My four sisters: Currie, Fane, Locha
and Minnie. and the Kid (the skinny
dude in the back).

Sisters Minnie and Fane...
early forties.

CHAPTER 11

LET THE GOOD TIMES ROLL!

In October of 1951, we moved to 1159 North Eleventh Street. At this time we were living in a garage that was on the property of a field contractor by the name of Gamboa. Living right next door to us, was my cousin Joe's family. An aunt of mine, Maria Lara Lomas, one of my father's sisters, was living with Joe's family at this time. My aunt was Joe's grandmother on his father's side. It was while at this "dwelling" that we used crates for our furniture; the same type of crate that we used out in the fields. My mother had my father stack up a series of these boxes vertically and, intermittently, horizontally, on top. These, across one wall of the garage, comprised her "china" cabinet. Around the perimeter of the garage, we placed some of these boxes on their side, or vertically, which provided for our "furniture." My favorite setup, not only here, but also out in the fields, was to lean one of the boxes against a wall (or a tree) and two or three boxes on the floor (or on the ground), the first of which was right up against the bottom edge of the leaning box; this providing an excellent "lounge" chair. This is what I used out in the fields at lunchtime, enjoying my mother's homemade burritos. In the middle of the garage lay a large mattress and other smaller means on which we slept. These times, harsh in many ways, were coming to an end; from this point on, my nomadic life was to change considerably.

It is here, on North Eleventh Street that my "growing up" years began. With my cousin living next door, he and I were about to embark on a journey of beautiful, early teen memories. Through this first semester of the eighth grade, Joe and I were best buddies and among the "big" guys on campus. My cousin Joe and I, along with newfound friends, were part of a "gang." The gang consisted of Joe Macias, his brother Tony, who was in high school at the time, Steve Pargas, with whom I had lived in Mendota, and who was a spectator at my "pencil poking" episode. The only other member I remember was a big, lovable guy by the name of Earnest Lara (no relation). Our gang activities consisted of hanging out at Backesto Park on

Thirteenth and Empire Street, which is very close to where we lived. We often went there to shoot some baskets, but mostly, we'd look for a flag football game. On Saturdays, we usually hung out at Peter Burnett Jr. High. This school had a real nice, indoor basketball court where we were always sure of engaging in a good basketball game. Elsewhere around San Jose, we would challenge other groups to a football game. These two sports occupied most of our free time, this and girls.

There was one event in which this "gang" of ours was involved, and which was not in line with our usual activities. One evening, we were hanging around just a few blocks from where we all lived and the streetlights came on. Well, this was too tempting and we all decided to take turns in putting one out. Picking rocks around us, we each took a turn. I don't remember who it was that finally hit the light, but I don't think the glass had hit the ground before we had all disappeared!

As I said, we all lived close by so we scattered in our respective directions, muy pronto! Joe Macias, his brother Tony, my cousin Joe, Ernest and I, all lived close to each other, so we all ran in the same direction. Big guy Earnest was the first to reach his house, which had a cyclone fence across the front yard. Grabbing the top of the fence while jumping over, Earnest had one of his fingers caught in the fence and while he made it over the fence, he was immediately, yanked back, having his finger tangled up. Earnest didn't break his finger, but it was momentarily bent something awful; I've had this experience when a soccer ball hit my finger squarely, only to have the PE coach take my hand in his, and with his other hand, pulled my finger back in place. Through this semester at Orchard, my cousin Joe and I spent most of our time together. This went on through the start of our sophomore year in high school, although Joe was attending San Jose High, while I was attending James Lick High.

While at Orchard, Joe and I had a field day with the girls; most boys did. It was a beautiful time for hundreds of boys and girls to go to the Jose Theatre every Saturday, sometimes requiring standing in line for quite a while, but it was well worth it. The routine was for us to go in and as soon as we adjusted to the darkness, start our quest for some girl's company. Having spotted a certain couple of girls, we would sit as close to them as we could, usually, a row or two behind. Initially, we would try to get their attention through body language; this not working, we would resort to "pitching" popcorn at them. If they responded in like kind, we knew we had gotten to first base. Thereafter, we'd spend the next hour or so "making out." These were not only enjoyable experiences, but also served as a "good neighbor" policy in that we got to know several girls from various schools in the surrounding San Jose area; these included Willow Glen, Santa Clara, Campbell and Los Gatos.

Two of these experiences that were not routine, are worthy of note. On one of these, the two girls we sat with had gotten to the theatre a lot earlier than Joe and I had. Therefore, they had to leave very shortly after just a short period of making out. Undaunted, and with time to seek out a new set of partners, Joe and I started from step one. Starting all over again, we tried to get the attention of two new girls by following our "patented" procedure. We soon made connection with two other girls, and this was the only time that either Joe or I, each got to enjoy the company of two different girls, on the same day. Good neighbor policy at its best!

The second unusual experience was very different and more of an ego booster for me. This time, a third buddy whom I do not remember, went with us. As we entered the Jose Theatre, I was leading the way, so that when we found an aisle with three available seats, I took the farthest one in, followed by Joe, then our friend. Once we got accustomed to the darkness, we spotted four girls two rows ahead of us. We started our routine in getting their attention and while a couple of them seemed interested, the leader of the pack was very annoyed, and let us know so. After a while, as we persisted with our mating call, the one girl got up and giving us a dirty look, left her seat with the other three girls following. They went and sat down one row further down, on the side aisle.

Very shortly thereafter, two seats were vacated directly in back of them and immediately, our friend, being closest to the aisle took off followed by Joe; being in the innermost seat, I was left behind. As soon as Joe and our friend sat down behind the girls, the one I was interested in looked back. I motioned to her to come sit with me, and to my surprise, she did. Because of this, this occasion was far more rewarding to me, and that Saturday afternoon, I walked out of the Jose Theater one proud dude! Outside, as we were walking away from the theater, my cousin Joe stated, "Boy, I can't believe you did that!" I didn't say anything, just had a silly grin on my face; after all, "war is war!"

While at Orchard Elementary, I made some new friends of whom several also went on to James Lick High. Among these, were Martha Cuenca, Dave Enos, Bob Lawrence, Joe Mora and Lois Ramirez. Each one of these friends was special to me, but Lois affected me much deeper. It was not a romantic kind of affection, although she is certainly among the most attractive girls I have ever known. Lois affected me with her special qualities; she has an amazingly beautiful personality; she is of "feet-on-the-ground" character, and she is as good a human being as anyone could hope to meet. She also happens to be quite a scholar.

That year, during the Christmas holidays, we went back to Del Rio, where I stayed to finish the eighth grade. Once again, I was reunited with my childhood friends. Our teacher, who had also been my teacher in the seventh grade, was Mr. Guardia, who is one of those dedicated teachers who show concern about his student's education. Although I have high regards for all of my teachers, Mr. Guardia is among my favorite. There is one incident, concerning Mr. Guardia, that I painfully regret and which I cannot erase, nor for which, I can ever forgive myself.

One day, while on the subject of History, Mr. Guadia asked me to read Lincoln's Gettysburg Address in front of the class and as I passed by him, he whispered, "Read it just as Lincoln did, I know you can do it." I retorted with, "I wasn't there, so I don't know how he read it." This didn't bother me right away, but as time went by I realized the stupidity of it, and worse, whenever I think of the utter disrespect for this teacher, who had so much confidence in me, and was only trying to encourage me, I cringe with shame, I really do. Looking at my report cards, Mr. Guardia gave me an "A" in the second semester of the seventh grade and an "A-" in the eighth grade; because of that stupid remark I made, I just can't feel good about these grades.

As I mentioned, through my earlier childhood years, I owed my good grades to Tony Treviño, Baby Calderon and Nani. Tony in particular, was instrumental through the seventh grade and my second semester in the eighth grade. Tony used to "oversee" a little surplus store his father ran, and here, we would do our homework, which was of real help to me. One afternoon, Baby was walking by the surplus store on her way home from school and stopped to visit with us. The three of us talked for a while and then, at Tony's "suggestion," Baby and I went inside and for the first time, I got my first real kiss; I was in love!

From this time on, through graduation, Baby and I were going "steady." She was to be my very first girlfriend. It was during this period of time that I wrote new lyrics to Tony Martin's popular song, "I get Ideas" for Baby. Further, with graduation pending,

I wrote to my mother, asking her to buy a ring as a graduation gift for Baby. I was real proud when I gave her that ring, and conversely, I was downhearted when I had to return to San Jose after graduation. This year was the last time I was to live in Del Rio; even my visits, which, at first had been on Christmas break, were to become less and less frequent.

CHAPTER 12

THE FIFTIES

My parents weren't at my eighth grade graduation. During my second semester of the eighth grade in Del Rio, they had moved in with my brother Chato, in San Jose. I joined them soon after graduating, and in the fall of 1952, while living there, I started my freshman year at James Lick. It was also while living at my brother's house that I bought my first car, a 1951 Chevy sedan.

My brother's house is still there, at 142 Pickford Avenue, except that it has been moved to the front of the property. When we lived there, the house was pretty much in the middle of the large lot, and I remember a large shade tree that not only provided coolness on hot days but was also my "get-away." I built a "tree house" on this tree and would sometimes do my homework up there, or simply just lie there and relax. I also had a fall that I'm sure has come to haunt me, in my old age. In the front yard, my brother had set up a swing set for the kids.

One weekend, my buddy, a fellow classmate, Eddie Payne, came over and we decided to remove the swings and the slide for an athletic undertaking. We wanted to see from how far away we could jump and still grab the cross member. We made a mark some distance away from the bar and then went back a certain distance from where we would take off. We kept increasing the mark distance until either one of us couldn't reach the bar. Since

Eddie is quite shorter than I am, he went out first. I increased the mark one more time and took off from a farther distance to gain more speed. I hit my mark and went flying through the air. I barely reached the bar with both hands, but my momentum was too great and my hands slipped just as my body was at the highest point and parallel to the ground. I hit the ground squarely on my back! I was a teenager and other than being momentarily stunned, I was not hurt then, but now the old body is remembering.

In discussing the summer we lived there, my sister Currie informed me that she, Locha and Dofo, had also lived at this house. For some reason, I was under the impression that these siblings of mine were already married and each living elsewhere. Even though the house was fairly large, I don't remember any one of them having lived at this house. As far as the logistics in this house, my brother and his wife, Paulina (Pauline) occupied the far end of the house, while we lived in the front portion, which included a small kitchen. According to Currie, my brother Dofo and I slept in a one-room cabin in the backyard. I do have memories of doing my homework in the dining room after school, or in the evenings. I also remember walking to and from school, mingling with school kids whom I did not yet know. Fortunately, my brother's house is less than a block from Hyland Avenue, from which, James Lick is only three blocks away. The campus itself is located on the corner of White Road and Alum Rock Avenue.

It was while living at my brother's house that I learned to drive. My father owned an early forties International pickup that is still a conversational piece amongst my friends who knew the truck well. When I first drove it, I stuck pretty close to our neighborhood, but eventually, I used to go pick up my cousin Joe, who at this time lived on North Fourth Street, a distance of about twelve miles.

The most challenging factor in driving "La Mala Mujer" (temperamental woman) as it was called, was the fact that the steering column was very, very loose. But, one adapts to any given vehicle and so it was with La Mala Mujer. Approaching a turn, I would start cranking the steering wheel by slapping it until it "caught" up and then, I could make the turn. This was an on-going experience that I had to deal with, but on the other hand, I was fourteen and I had "wheels."

After I had learned to drive, I used to borrow my brother Dofo's car occasionally. On one such occasion, when I had gone over to visit my cousin Joe, a Policeman stopped me on the way back home. The windshield on my brother's car had a jagged crack traversing the entire passenger side, and this is what the officer pointed out to me. He simply stated that I should have it fixed and let me go; I didn't have a license.

I n my sophomore year at James Lick, I bought my first car; it was a '51 Chevy sedan. Eddie, my high school pal, just reminded me of the time when he came over and helped me put a bag of cement in the trunk so as to "lower" the car. In addition, I asked him to stand on the rear bumper while I took a profile photo of my "low rider." This car, too, had its idiosyncrasy; every time I came to a stop, the gear linkage would lock up. I would get out of the car, rush over and open the hood and yank the linkage loose. This worked every time and this too, was "adaptable."

Eddie tells me of a comical "car theft" incident. In the fifties, it was a happenstance of the times to steal hubcaps. "moons" were very popular. Anyway, Eddie and my brother used to be drinking buddies and on one such outing, Eddie tells me my brother Dofo came into the bar excitedly proclaiming to Eddie to come and check out the hubcaps he had just gotten. We'll, it turned out that my father was also a drinking buddy with Eddie, and on this occasion, my brother had unknowingly "stolen" my father's hubcaps! Just for the record, I'm not a drinking man, and with the exception of a couple of childhood "indiscretions, I have never stolen anything.

Later, in summer of 1952, my mother bought a little house directly across the street from my brother's house; the address is 135 Pickford Avenue. This tiny little house became the focal point for family gatherings; it is still spoken of as if it were a shrine. This is because of the warmth and love my mother bestowed on us; she instilled in us that social element called "family unity." This little house had three rooms and one bathroom. It had a full, front porch, with the front door leading to the paneled front room. Directly ahead of the front room was a small bedroom and to the left, the kitchen. To the right of the kitchen, and down a short hall, was the bathroom. A door at the end of the hall led to a long backyard that had a plum tree and an almond tree at the far end, both of which my son fondly remembers. My father also had a goat, and some chickens in the backyard, which all the children enjoyed on family visits.

There was a loquat t tree in the front yard that had special meaning to all of us. This tree became an icon, symbolic of the love and respect we had for my mother and father, and for this little house; I looked forward to its fruit every season and took some home in hopes of growing my own loquat tree, knowing it had come from my mother's yard. It is almost comical how much respect we had for my mother. From my brother Dofo on up, and including my brothers-in law, none of them would smoke in front of my mother. On one family gathering at this tiny house, while the women were in the house visiting, and the children playing the backyard, the men were gathered on the front yard, smoking and drinking. At an unexpected moment, my mother came out onto the porch to call us in for dinner. Immediately, the beer cans went into hiding and the cigarettes discretely dropped to the ground, or were cupped into a folded hand. I'm always amused whenever I think of this little "gotcha!" My mother just walked back into the house amused by the incident. She certainly knew the grown men smoked and drank; yet, I understood their reaction; it was one of pure respect.

Not long after we had moved into my mother's house, we got the news that my oldest brother, Jose, had died in a tragic accident in Del Rio. The fact that my brother had died was kept from my mother so that she could eventually prepare for, and accept, the bad news. She was told that he was in serious condition and may not make it. We borrowed someone's car to make the trip to Del Rio, and I believe it was my brother, Chato's car. On the day we were to leave, my father could not keep the truth from my mother any longer and just came out and told her. The pain that she was carrying already may have cushioned that final blow. She was crying and sadly lamented, "I know, I knew it already." In her heart and in her mind, she had seen through all of us.

What made the tragedy worse, was the fact that my brother was on his way to my sister, Minnie's house about a family matter. Concerned with whatever the matter was, my brother, Jose was going over to my sister to confront her with this situation.

Just a few blocks from his house, which was not far from my sister's house on Esquivel, my brother suffered a heart attack. What pains me the most about this unfortunate tragedy, is the fact that his two young sons, Papi (Jose Jr) and Beto (Roberto) witnessed the car crash. They were playing at a "park" which was no more than an empty, square block lot. It did have a swing and slide on which my nephews were playing.

The younger son was the first to see their father's car coming in their direction. He pointed this out to his older brother and at that time, they saw the car swerve onto the wrong lane and watched as the car picked up speed and crash through a telephone pole at the far corner of the park. For some time, we thought that the accident had killed my brother, but although it most probably would have, the report was that he had suffered a heart attack. This was the first death in our family that I experienced and the first time I cried in public.

Through the remainder of the year, and well into the school year, Eddie and I became very close friends. Ironically, another new friend at Lick was Tony Barrera who turns out to be a cousin of the Barrera brother and sister that had come with us to California in 1946. The three of us I still meet for breakfast now and then, but only occasionally, as Eddie is quite a rover. Both Eddie and Tony happen to be from Del Rio, a fact that I wasn't aware of until our second year at James Lick. Eddie and I lived three and a half blocks from James Lick, he, directly south from school and I, directly east. In our freshman year, after school, we would each run home and whoever got to his house first, would call the other to confirm the "winner." Because of his speed, Eddie used to be called "Flash" in Del Rio, but I was no slack myself in the speed department, although, I don't remember who won those silly races; it was just a teenage way to kill time. On one other occasion, Eddie and I, along with another classmate, Chris Trujillo, decided to run as far as we could up Alum Rock Avenue towards Alum Rock Park, a distance of about four miles. Our starting point was the creamery, a very nostalgic hangout for the James lick crowd. The creamery was located at the corner of White Road and Alum Rock Avenue, kitty corner from the James Lick parking lot. I was the first to run out of gas, then Eddie; Chris was very strong and had a lot of stamina. Eddie tells me that Chris is still working, his line of work being in construction. I'm sure that if not for Eddie and me, Chris would have made it all the way to the park without any rest stops.

Through the first three years at James Lick, I continued to work in the fields during the summer months. This was something many school kids did. Mostly, the boys picked apricots, cherries and pears, while more commonly, girls worked at cutting apricots. This involved cutting apricots in half and lining the halves in rows on a wooden tray that, when full, would be stacked on top of another, until several trays were stacked. This set of stacks would then be taken to the drying shed. The drying shed was some distance from the cutting area, but the smell of sulfur could be detected through the cutting area and for some distance beyond.

Picking apricots, pears and cherries provided spending money for us teenagers. It afforded us school clothes, shoes and cruising money on Thursdays. Thursdays were special in that, this was the only day of the week that stores stayed open until 9 P.M. I remember when all stores closed at 5 P.M. on weekdays, and closed on Sundays. Downtown San Jose was always crowded with teenage shoppers on Thursday evenings, and the streets were filled with '50s cars, cruising. Cruising took place along First Street from San Salvador at the south edge of downtown, north to Santa Clara Street. From the corner of First and Santa Clara, we turned east to Second Street, from which we turned south, back to San Salvador, and start all over again. This is one of the most fun activities for us teenagers in the fifties, this and the drive-in hamburger places, and certainly, the drive-in theaters!

The cherry and apricot orchards I worked at during the summers, were mostly located along Capitol Avenue, north of McKee Road. This part of San Jose is now heavily residential, with the northernmost part of Capitol Avenue, where once stood the Ford Plant, now engulfed by a very large shopping mall appropriately named, "The Great Mall." Picking pears was mostly done in the Alviso area and this too, was fun.

One summer, a cousin of mine, Benny Montez and I, were picking pears in this area. This particular day was very hot and just after lunch we were quite "sluggish". Once again, to pass the time away and to snap ourselves out of our slumber, we started playing "catch" with some very overripe pears. This kept us entertained for a while, but my cousin eventually got too sleepy and decided to snooze. Standing on the ladder and resting his head on his arms at the top of the ladder, Benny dozed off. As tired as I was, and sleepy-headed also, I could not take a "nap" on short notice. A few minutes into the napping session, I saw, too late, the field supervisor approaching. He called Benny down from his ladder and gave him what-for; we were both fired, right on the spot. Cousin Benny had a very successful career at Lockheed; he was also in the Engineering Services, which was my line of work. I was quite shocked to hear that my cousin passed away recently. I heard that he had died of cancer, this in Oregon, where he had been living for several years.

There is one incident involving an apricot- picking weekend

that two friends of mine and I still talk about whenever we swap memories of those picking days. This one incident involved Eddie Payne, Tony Barrera, along with Chris Trujillo and his brother, Alex, and also, my brother in law, Gabriel, or "Chacho," as he was called. Except for my brother in-law, the others and I were going to James Lick at the time, probably in my sophomore year. Ironically, the orchard was located in the Almaden Valley, very close to where I was to buy a "mini" ranch, years later. Again, to pass the time away, we swapped jokes, sang (or attempted to sing) songs of the day. And of course, there was the usual "rotten" apricot toss. The song, Crying In The Chapel was popular at that time and Alex kept singing it off and on throughout the morning, which was a respite from the drudgery of the work, and which, in fact, he actually did a pretty good job.

Just about lunchtime, this annoying, loud noise alerted us to the fact that it was, in fact, lunchtime; unknown to us, Chacho carried with him an alarm clock that was set just for such a purpose. Never before, through my years of working in the fields, had anyone brought an alarm clock to the fields. We could not stop laughing at my brother-in-law for having brought that clock to work, and, I guess, waking us up.

The other incident involved Eddie and Tony. As mentioned before, we'd clown around in different ways just to make the time go by faster. On this occasion, at lunchtime, Tony dozed off and Eddie took advantage of the situation. He carefully removed Tony's shoes and hid them. When lunchtime was over, we all had a good laugh, as Tony, panicky, was looking for his shoes. These are silly, little memories, but they are part of the nostalgia.

Working in the summers was part of the fifties scene, which in many cases involved washing dishes at any one of the popular drive-in restaurants. Through this time, although we were living with our parents, most of us kids paid our own way. The money we earned through the summers went for school clothes, shoes and dating. Now, I could afford to buy more than one pair of shoes per school year and I didn't have to wear any one of them down to the sole. We still never had enough money though. Whenever we went cruising downtown, my buddies and I would chip in with any change we could spare. The gas at that time was thirty-two cents a gallon, and occasionally, we would drive a few miles towards Morgan Hill where this gas station had gas at nineteen cents a gallon! Now you know why I say that era of fifties may never come again. The summer work also afforded me the money with which to buy the 1951 Chevy, while at my brother's house. That period, through the fifties, was the last of the good times, a time of innocence, a time of values and of family unity.

Although I was a freshman at James Lick High, and my cousin Joe was a freshman at San Jose High, we still palled around that year and into the beginning of our sophomore year. Only, by now, we had outgrown the Jose Theater crowd and were now going to the main theatres in town, the UA and The California. Both of these theaters were fancy and upscale, with the California being very ornate in its decor. One Saturday mid-afternoon, my life was re-directed in a most profound way. My cousin Joe and I were leaving the theater, I believe it was the UA, when, as we turned left towards Santa Clara Street, we saw a young couple coming towards us. Aware that there was a young man walking beside the girl, I actually didn't notice him at all; I was completely mesmerized by the beauty of the young girl at his side. As we got closer, both my heart and my brain were racing rapidly. I had never see a more beautiful girl than the one coming towards me. Because of her poise and her demeanor, I sized her to be older than I. I remember thinking, "She's probably eighteen, or nineteen."

As we were passing by each other, she gave me a smile that just about knocked me out of my shoes! Old Cupid must have been out of arrows, or else he forgot his bow, because I felt as if he had picked up one of the street light poles and jammed it right through my chest! If anyone doesn't believe in love at first sight, believe me, it exists. A couple of steps further, I looked back over my shoulder, and she too, was looking back over her shoulder. At this point, I elbowed my cousin, repeating, "Did you see that! Did you see that?" My cousin had a pensive look on his face and then said the magic words, " I've seen that girl before; I know her from somewhere."

Close to two weeks later, during which time I had pestered him to remember, the memory of the girl had started to fade a little, but the feelings hadn't. The next time I saw cousin Joe, he told me he remembered who the girl was. He also had a class picture of his younger sister, which among the students was this pretty, doe-eyed, cherubic girl; her name was Gloria. Well, now I knew who this girl was, this girl who had stolen my heart and hadn't returned it. But of what value was this? San Jose has many schools, and then, there are the suburbs of Willow Glen, Campbell, Santa Clara and Los Gatos; she could be going to school at any one of these places! Well, a few more weeks went by and the memory of that vision I had encountered was diminishing. Then, one day, during break, I was having a soda at the quad when Tony Barrera came by and very excitedly said, "Rudy, you have to see this freshman girl! She's the prettiest girl you've ever seen!" Well, we proceeded down the exterior corridor towards the freshman wing and stood across from the front double doors, waiting for the bell to ring. Within a minute or two, the bell rang and out came what seemed like a wave of various shapes of multi-colors and multi-sizes, all, seemingly in slow motion. It seemed to me, momentarily, like a Van Gough painting. The only face that was vividly clear among this blurred mass was that same girl I had seen downtown some weeks before; it was Gloria! How prophetic of Tony to say that this would b the most beautiful girl I had ever seen! I had known that, weeks ago!

Once again, as Gloria turned in front of us, she gave me that patented smile of hers, only this time it was followed by a "Hi!" I responded "Hi" and my eyes followed her as she walked away. At this point, I experienced one of those "movie" scenes,

144

where we see a couple late at night in an apartment, and behind them, through the window, we see the neon lights of businesses across the street and the lights of a few cars passing by. Then, the scene "fades" out and then fades back in to early morning. The man is reading the paper, while the woman pours him a cup of coffee. Outside, it is daylight and very little traffic is seen. In my case, the last thing I am aware of, concerning that first meeting with Gloria, is watching her disappear into the distance, mingling with the masses, on her way to the next class. I wish I could remember the look on Tony's face when Gloria said "Hi!" I don't even remember walking back with Tony, nor do I remember anything else about the rest of that day. Like the movie scene I made up, the next thing I remember is standing back in front of the freshman wing the next day, only this time, I was alone.

This time, the mass of freshmen was clear, and the motion was normal. When Gloria came out, I immediately fell in step with her, to which she asked, "Where are you going?" I quickly replied, "I'm walking you to your class, if that's alright with you." She smiled and asked, "Won't you be late to your class?" "It's only an elective, not a core subject," I replied. The rest, as they say, is history.

From that day on, through her three years at James Lick, Gloria and I were inseparable. The very first time I kissed Gloria, was in the back seat of a 1957 Chevy Bel Air that belonged to a cousin of mine, who happened to be driving. Eddie was sitting in front, while my other cousin, Joe, sat in the back with us. We were on the way to a party at a house belonging to an uncle of one of my close buddies from James Lick, Jim Johnson. Jim lived directly across the street from Eddie on Hobart, which is off White Road. These two had known each other for some time before I met either one. Every now and then, I stop by at Jim's Auto," an auto shop he and his son run.

On our return to school in my junior year, while walking Gloria to her class, Mrs. Lois Hardy, who had been my freshman homeroom teacher, saw us and commented, "Looks like you two are the only ones that summer didn't break up!" My grades, in more than one class, suffered once our courtship got underway. Prior to that, in my freshman year, I had signed up for Algebra 1. I knew it was a math course, but I really didn't know what it was about, but still got a "B."

Along with the required courses and Algebra 1, I took French 1, and General Art. That first year, I had ten "A's" and four "B's" including a summer course in Typing. I still did well through most of my sophomore year, getting eight "A's", three "B's" and my first "C" in Geometry, this, in the second semester, whereas, I had gotten an "A" the first semester. This was the beginning of the decline in my good grades.

In my junior year, I didn't get one "A" and I got my first "F", this in Algebra 11, in which I redeemed myself in my senior year by getting a "B." I got the "B" in this class by sacrificing my grade in Spanish 111, which I was flunking. I had gotten an "A" in Spanish the first semester, but the reason I was in danger of flunking it in the second semester, was that I had been doing my Algebra homework through most of the semester. My Spanish class teacher, Miss Bouret, had let me get away with it, but informed me that in order for me to pass, I was to "coach" a group of students in preparing for a play in Spanish for the final. I spent the last two weeks of the semester coaching the "cast" and thus, I sneaked in with a "D."

Although my grades suffered greatly as a result of my courting Gloria, I was fortunate in having taken a few courses that were to define my life's work. These were the three math courses, four years of Art and in particular, my two years in Industrial Art. All of these courses were to be very instrumental in my line of work. One other, very important course that comes into play, regardless of the profession, is English. Because of my sluggish beginnings in this subject, I made it a concentrated effort to learn it well. As for P.E., in spite of my lanky, skinny physic, I did very well in this subject, averaging a "B+" throughout the four years.

Although I had some athletic ability and did well in most PE activities, I didn't have the discipline or the drive that is necessary to participate in organized sports. The varsity head coach, Ed Alluigie asked Gloria to talk me into going out for the football team. Feeling proud that the coach felt I might have some talent, and the fact that he asked my girlfriend to get me to sign up, I did just that. After a couple of weeks of practice, I could see the drive most of the players had. One of the players with whom I was competing for the wide receiver position, was nicknamed "Stretch." He was much taller than I, and heavier. He definitely had what it took to play organized sports and went on to play football and basketball through his four years at James lick. He went to college on a scholarship in these sports.

On one of the practices, the coach was showing us proper "stance," and he happened to walk by me when he kicked my legs out from under me, yelling out, "Spread them farther apart!" I fell on my face. The humiliation and the fact that I didn't have the "hunger," changed my mind about trying out, so I quit the team, which I was to regret, because I loved to play football. Ironically, Stretch broke his leg on the first game and was out for the season. I feel confident that had I stayed on, I would have replaced him, at least for that year.

In my freshman year, in PE, there were two athletic events of which I am very proud; these involved a basketball tournament and another tournament consisting of a variety of gymnastics events along with a couple of track-and-field events. The basketball tournament involved teams that were made up of a fair mix of all class levels, from freshmen to seniors. The other tournament, involving gymnastics, was first and took place during my freshman year. The events were all based on individual achievement, and most of the events took place in the gym. The "trophy" at the end of the tournament, was that we got to wear gold trunks. Starting out wearing white trunks, which were referred to as "hamburger whites," the difficulty of the events increased, either in time or in number, as we worked our way to the "gold." After the white trunks, came red, then blue, followed by green, and finally, the gold trunks.

Among the toughest events for me through each level were the parallel bars and the rope climb. The only way I managed to do the rope climb, was to shut my mind off to the "impossibility" attitude that was blocking my mind, and to just go ahead and do it. I could not manage to do the same for the parallel bars, which required jumping in between the bars and with pure arm strength, doing eighteen lifts. If not for having failed this event, I would have gotten my gold trunks as a freshman; no one got their gold trunks that year. At the end of the year, coach Alliguie signed my yearbook, "Let's see you get the gold trunks next year." I did get my gold trunks as a sophomore and I did it by psyching my self up to do twenty-five repetitions instead of the eighteen required; this after a good friend bet me that I couldn't do it, actually, an act of encouragement on his part. Ironically, the only other person who got his gold trunks that year, was the same student that my team was to beat in the basketball tournament that came later.

At the start of the basketball tournament, captains were assigned, of which I was one. Each captain chose a team that included a member from each class with my team consisting of a junior, two sophomores and a freshman; I was a sophomore. As I recall, there were four teams involved and towards the end of the tournament, my team was tied for first place with one other team. The captain of this team was a junior, and also first string on the school "B" basketball team; he was the only other student who had gotten the gold trunks earlier.

The day before the play-off game, I got sick and didn't go to school the following day; that is, I did not attend any of my classes except for P.E.; I didn't want to let my team down, especially since we were tied for first place. On top of my feeling sick, one of my team members had also reported sick that day and so we wound up with only four players; sounds like "Rocky," doesn't it? Initially, the captain of the other team protested because we didn't have a full roster. Coach Ed Alliguie asked me if I wanted to play anyway, to which I replied, "Yes." So, with one man short, the game was on. It was a grueling game for me, in that, physically, it took a lot more out of me having to play without a full roster. Finally, and barely, my team won! The captain of the other team protested once more, this time because he had found out that I was technically not in school. He pointed out to the coach that I had missed all my other classes. Coach Alliguie, being a coach of true grit, responded, "If it meant that much to him, it's okay with me!"

As mentioned before, my grades through my four years at James Lick, were above average. Right after graduation, with nothing else but these grades, I went out to apply for a job as a Junior Draftsman at FMC (Food Machinery Corporation). My two years of Algebra and one of Geometry, along with my two years of Industrial Art, were actually the courses that were relevant to drafting. Throughout my two years in Mr. Rufus Tucker's Industrial Arts class, he would occasionally point out to the class the various opportunities in Drafting as a profession, and the different levels one could work up to; he himself, worked at FMC as a Design Checker during the summers.

On the very last day of my senior year in Mr. Tucker's class, he bid us farewell and best wishes as he handed out the report cards. He asked me to hold back, saying he had something to tell me. After the last student had left, Mr. Tucker said, "Rudy, I just wanted to let you know that you were the only student in any of my classes this year, that got an "A." I had gotten "A's" in other classes, but, concerning my schooling, this has got to be the best compliment I ever received.

CHAPTER 13

GOOD-BY, JAMES LICK

Leaving James Lick High School has been a bittersweet, life-long experience. It was such a major factor in my life in that, the experience took place right through the heart of the fifties, an era most beautiful in the history of America.

Right after graduating from James Lick, and armed with nothing else but my diploma and relevant courses, I went out to apply for the position of Junior Draftsman at Food Machinery Corporation (FMC). Quite nervous, and not without some fear, I approached the personnel counter. I stated that I was looking for a job in drafting, to which, the lady replied, "There are no openings in Drafting." Momentarily stunned, and just to save face, I asked if I could fill out an application. "If you want to, but there are no openings in Drafting," she reiterated. Feeling downtrodden, I went and sat down to fill out the application, which consisted of nothing more than my personal information, and my high school courses.

Just as I had completed the application, I heard a familiar voice; it was Mr. Tucker! "Hey, Rudy! What brings you here?" Mr. Tucker had a slow, drawl to his speech, a combination of Will Rogers and W.C. Fields. I had forgotten that Mr. Tucker worked at FMC during the summers, and at this very moment, he had just gotten through with his personnel paperwork. I told him my situation, and he said, "Let me have the application, and I'll see what I can do." Two weeks after I had graduated from James Lick, I was working as a Junior Drafter at FMC, one of the top employers at that time! Mr. Tucker's kind recommendation embarked me on a forty-five year career in Engineering Services.

Six months after Gloria graduated from James Lick, we got married on December 15, 1957. For those six months, she had attended San Jose State University on a Business scholarship. My cousin Joe was one of my groomsmen, as was Amador Urrabazo, one of the twins that had come to California with us on that first journey. My best friend, Eddie Payne, would have certainly been one of my groomsmen, if not my best man, but he was in the service at this time. I found out years later that as a junior, in one of his classes, Eddie had taken his snoozing, teacher's shoes, and thrown them onto the roof.

On another occasion, Eddie tells me, he tied the same snoozing teacher's shoestrings together; only this time, he was taken to the Principal's office where he was rightfully reprimanded. On the way to the principal's office, Eddie came upon a couple of friends that were also going to the Principal's office on unrelated circumstances. That same day, Eddie and the two others, impulsively left school and went to register for the Armed Services; I didn't see Eddie again for over fifteen years.

On the wedding day, while my groomsmen and I were getting dressed, and in the confusion, my cousin Joe and I inadvertently switched shirts. Well, Joe had a physique like the actor Clint Walker, a small waist, and a big upper body. Through the wedding ceremony, my cousin was very uncomfortable, as the shirt was too tight on his neck. Meanwhile, I could have done a 180-degree turn in his shirt, as I was on the slender side. We laughed about it after the wedding and traded shirts at the first opportunity.

The first place Gloria and I lived at was at 1145 Shortridge Avenue, one short block south of Santa Clara Street, off Twenty Fourth Street. We had a room on the second floor of a fairly new apartment complex. Although our rent was less than $80 per month, we were struggling financially on my meager salary. I was getting $216 per month before taxes. We did have my 1956 Mercury Montclair and the basic furniture, but with the deductions, the utilities, groceries and miscellaneous expenses, we barely made it. I remember some times when we scraped pennies to go to the Mayfair Theater, which was just around the corner on Santa Clara Street. At another point in our early marriage, I remember taking seventy-five silver dollars that we were saving and had to use them to pay the utilities.

Before Gloria reached the age of nineteen, she was hired at Lockheed Sunnyvale as a file clerk and financially, this turned things around for us. We didn't know at the time she was hired, that she was pregnant, and she continued to work very close to the due date. Our son, Robert, was born on February 23, 1959 after more than a few hours before the delivery. He took his time coming into this world, weighing almost ten pounds. I was one proud father; here was our first- born, and it was a boy!

This new responsibility presented experiences that all new parents face, and which we all learn on "the fly." For one thing, our social life was drastically curtailed. A simple thing like going to the Mayfair Theater, presented a problem; now we had a hungry and loudly, whining infant with us. It became prudent for us to sit up in the balcony, this to minimize the noise and also where Gloria could feed our son in privacy. Our next-door neighbors at the apartment also suffered. One time, around three-thirty in the morning, Bob was crying his lungs out and the neighbors began banging on the wall; I took the mattress off the bed and dragged it to the front room, where the three of us slept for some time, thereafter.

We bought our first house in a brand new development, towards the end of 1959. The house was located on a corner lot at 598 Coyote Road, the other street being Symphony Lane. The "American Dream" had come true for us; we had our own home, on a corner lot, and yes, a white picket fence out front. We lived at this house for approximately ten years, where our son attended Christopher Elementary into the second grade. That school was across Coyote Road, and less than two blocks away from our house.

A twist of irony and a horrible experienced occurred while living at the Coyote Road address. Once Bob and Ruby were able to play outside, I was vigilant in protecting them from harm, principally, every parent's fear, crossing a street. With Bob, when he was just a toddler, I would take him out in front of the house, on the sidewalk, and roll volleyball towards him. He would pick it up and roll it back to me. Then, making sure there were no cars coming, even though this was a brand new development and very little traffic went through, I would roll the ball off the sidewalk onto the street and tell Bob to get it. He hesitated, but he minded. When he returned the ball, I gave him a gentle swat on the behind and told him never to go onto he street without first making sure that no cars were coming.

Of course he was confused; he had obeyed me. I hugged him and told it was OK and continued our little game. I did this one more time, with Bob being a little more hesitant the second time, but once again, he obeyed. I gave him another swat and this time I told him that no matter who told him to go after a ball on the street, that he was not to do so; and I stressed that even if I told him to go retrieve a ball, that he was not to do so. I then hugged him again and explained my concern for him.

This worked almost to a comical extent in that both he and Ruby, when crossing the street, would stand on the edge of the sidewalk and look and look in both directions, even though the street was absolutely clear of any traffic. Then, one day when Bob was a little older, he was playing with the next-door neighbor's son, who was Bob's age. They were tossing a boomerang and it errantly went across the street. Bob did what he had learned well, and then crossed the street to retrieve the boomerang. Before crossing the street back, he saw a car coming that was so far away, he could have easily crossed the street twice; but he was following my instructions to the letter.

A young, Samaritan was driving the car and stopped to let my son cross; but Bob wouldn't. Finally, the young man got out and assured my son that it was OK, even guiding him across. What Bob and the young man didn't see was a car coming from the opposite direction; the sun, setting directly in line with the street, blinded their vision.

My son saw the car too late and as he tried to turn away from it, the driver also turned away from Bob. Nevertheless, the car struck Bob and threw him a few feet forward. My wife, Gloria and I witnessed this from our living room and rushed out to our son. It was a horrible experience. Bob was saying that he couldn't breath; one of his shoes had come off on impact and he had a few scratches on his foot.

In panic, we did what one is instructed not to do. We brought out a blanket and covered Bob up. I then carried him into the house; we just could not accept our son lying in the gutter, where he had landed. Fortunately, he was not seriously hurt. His running in the opposite direction and behind a small trees in our front yard, plus the driver turning away from Bob; the driver hit Bob and the tree simultaneously. Ironically, my worst fears for my children's safety came to reality.

An unfortunate, sideline to this story is that one of our neighbors, who happened to know my sister Locha, called her and told her of the accident. My sister, in her panic to get to the hospital, ran into a closet door and got a very nasty gash on her forehead. In fact, at the hospital, our doctor saw that my sister need more immediate attention then our son and took care of her first. She was not seriously hurt either.

On June 23, 1962, our daughter Ruby was born. Unlike Bob, Ruby was more than eager to face the world. I remember the morning Gloria was cleaning house in the master bedroom, while I was taking out the garbage. Just as I walked back into the bedroom, Gloria folded over in pain. "It's time," she said. I rushed outside to the car, taking the small suitcase Gloria had at the ready. I threw the suitcase in the backseat, left the passenger-side door open and ran back in to get Gloria. She was trying to remain calm, but obviously in pain. I was in pretty bad shape myself, but knew what I had to do. I picked her up and carried her to the car, reversed out of the driveway very rapidly, and sped off, up Coyote road.

Now, Ruby also gave me a scare when she was in grade school. I was in the living room, lying down on the floor, watching TV. Bob came running into the living room and exclaiming that Ruby was choking. I jumped up, or tried too, falling back down. Then I ran onto the hallway, slipped and fell again! By this time Ruby came in from the kitchen and by this time, her throat had cleared.

It seems that she and Bob were mixing a chocolate drink and Ruby thought to take a spoonful of dry chocolate and inhaled a bunch of it. After some agonizing moments, while I was falling all over the place, her own saliva eventually diluted the chocolate and she was able to swallow. I thank God that those were the only scary experiences concerning my son and daughter, because I'm just not good at these things!

Coyote Road comes to a tee with Senter Road, five blocks away. At this tee, there is a stop sign, which I went through. Turning right, Senter also leads to a tee, approximately five miles north, to where Story Road, coming from east San Jose, changes into Keyes; at this juncture, I turned left. Between Coyote Road and Keyes, there are several stop signs, all of which I went through. At the tee with Story and Keyes, there is a traffic light. About a quarter of a mile before reaching this traffic light, I had been driving on the wrong side of the road, passing slower traffic on my lane, wildly honking the horn all the time. I got to the tee while I was still on the wrong lane and with the red light against me, went through this one, also.   Throughout   this driving ordeal, Gloria was going through a horrible ordeal of her own. She was screaming in pain, saying that she couldn't hold it anymore. I, very panicky by this time, kept telling her that we were almost there, pleading with her to hold on. After going through the red light and turning left on Keyes, I immediately turned right onto Twelfth Street. This street leads to Santa Clara Street, on which the hospital is located, two blocks east. I don't think I ran any more lights while on Santa Clara Street; I just remember turning left on Fourteenth and immediately parking in front of the hospital.

I carried Gloria into the lobby, desperately calling out, "We need a wheelchair!" It so happened that a nurse was just coming out of an elevator with a wheelchair. Quickly, I sat Gloria in the wheelchair and the nurse, just as quickly, took her up the elevator. Relieved that we had made it to the hospital, I went out to the car to bring in the suitcase. Back at the counter, I proceeded to fill out the required information and just as I had finished, the nurse was coming out of the elevator proclaiming, "Congratulations! You have a daughter!" The delivery took about twenty minutes from the time we got there! The little bundle of joy born that day was to be my little "Tweekart" and to this day, she still is. I was twenty-six years old when this blessed event came to be; Gloria was twenty-three. Both Gloria's and my career were on the rise, we had a new home, a son and a daughter, and out pet dog, a German shepherd that we named Prince. The Kid from Del Rio was riding high! I can't tell you how proud, how fortunate I felt, but most of all, how thankful I was.

I believe it was 1967 when we bought our second house, this one, in the Blossom Hill area, this area being a little nicer, and being surrounded by the Santa Teresa hills, just blocks from our new house. This area had a shopping mall, grade schools, two high schools and a hospital, all less than three miles from our house. There was, and still is, a Shell gas station that is owned by a very good human being, known to me as Jerry. A couple of times, when I had car trouble, I called Jerry at the gas station and he came over to my house to help me out. Although I don't usually use Shell gasoline, now and then when I do stop by, Jerry greets me with "Hi, Ruben!" It's nice to have businesses like Jerry's Shell in the neighborhood.

When we bought this second house, we were able to select the lot from the planning map, and while the house was under construction, we would go by and see it come to life. When the "shell" of the house had been completed, we went in and took a tour around the unfinished interior; it was difficult to visualize the individual rooms, as it was yet, just a maze of framing. As noted before, our first house at 598 Coyote Road was on a corner with Symphony Lane. The new house, at 6226 Drifter Drive, was on a corner with Cozy Drive; Coyote-Symphony and Cozy-Drifter; I find this to be ironically amusing. It was a t the Drifter house that we bought Bob a Honda Mini-bike for Christmas; he was ten at the time. The condition for the bike was that he cleared out all the weeds along the curb. He got a hoe and chopped them down but certainly, did not clear them. He enjoyed his bike, riding up in the Santa Teresa Hills. I got to ride it also, before going to work. I used to go with him on his paper route, which was very early in the morning. It was also while living at Drifter that Ruby was to begin her own little zoo...cats, dogs, mice; it was a zoo!

The price tag on the Coyote house was a whopping $13,750 in 1959! The price tag on the Drifter house was an amazingly, monstrous $25,500 in 1969! I make jest of this because the house I now own, not much bigger than the Coyote house, has a price tag close to $700,000! Just like the price of gas today, we'll never see home prices like we had in the good old days. Looking back at the prices at which we bought those two homes, not even the cost of the Drifter house would qualify for a down payment on any house, at today's prices!

Although, a point in fact: Even in 1959, when we bought the first house, we couldn't have bought it without help. We wouldn't have qualified if it hadn't been for Gloria's father (actually, step-father, Ish Padilla, who had adopted her as a baby). He bought our house under his name with his Cal-Vet, and after a year, or so, grant-deeded it to us. We were able to qualify for the Drifter house, on the other hand, as we both had good incomes at this time, plus the fact that, owning the Coyote house generated additional, rental income.

It was while my first wife, Gloria and I were living at the Drifter house, on November 18,1975, that we got the news that my next oldest brother, Chato, had died, also unexpectedly, as had my brother Jose, and unfortunately, under similar circumstances.

That day, my brother had gone over to visit a friend and while there, wasn't feeling well. Concerned, the friend asked if my brother wanted to be taken to the hospital, but my brother said no. This friend called my sister-in-law, Paulina to have someone come pick up my brother but by that time, he felt well enough and drove himself home. Arriving at home, my brother walked up to the front door, and upon entering the house, he fell forward and died of a massive heart attack. Johnny, the youngest son, was at the door to greet his father and, tried to revive him, but to no avail.

Four years later, we received news that any son or daughter dreads; my mother had passed away. Gloria and I were getting ready for work and the kids ready for school. I was walking downstairs when the phone rang and Gloria answered it. She came out of our bedroom and just said, "Ruben, your mother died." I was not quite down the stairs and just sat down, very bewildered. I remember thinking, "Who am I going to turn to now." I felt very alone that instant.

My mother had been ill for several years with asthma, or possibly with what was not heard of then, second-hand smoke. My father was a chain smoker throughout all his life, and perhaps this was a contributor to her condition. While she was in the hospital, I used to go see her at lunchtime and we'd talk, mostly her asking me about my kids. When it was determined that nothing more could be done for her, she opted to go home. My sister, Currie took her to her house and cared for her for the next few weeks that she was to live.

As a little boy, I used to cry at the thought of my mother dieing. Even as a young boy and into my teenage years, I would cringe at the thought and even shake my head to remove the thought. She was an extraordinary woman; she was compassionate, perhaps to a fault. Love, kindness and caring; those were her trademarks; and she was such a tiny woman, yet with so much to give. Judy and I visit her and my father every Memorial Day, Christmas, Easter or periodically on a weekend. Judy's grandmother, Pearl is also buried at Oak Hill Cemetery, and of course, we visit her each time also.

The death of my brother and that of my mother's dampened Gloria's and my lives, but the fact that we were in good health and raising our own family, eventually made it easier to go on. Once again, we had relocated to another, brand-new community. We were making good money, had a 1965 Ford Mustang, good tenants paying for the Coyote house, and two fantastic children, who, to this day, continue to be fantastic adults; although, it's a shame kids can't stay kids forever. By this time, I had left FMC after six years and had gone to work at Lockheed, Sunnyvale, where Gloria was still working, and from where she was to retire after a successful career some thirty-two years later. She went from starting out as a file clerk to Administrative Secretary for one of the top chiefs in the company's Security Department.

An interesting story concerning my move to Lockheed: I would probably have stayed at FMC throughout my career if not for a fellow co-worker of mine, Lou Jaramillo. He reminds me of a James Cagney type; both similar in stature and in dynamic personality. Lou came up to me one day and told me that we could get more money at Lockheed, and that the company was hiring. We took off one day, armed with a few resumes, and headed to Lockheed, where we dropped off our resumes and filled out an application. From there, we went to at least two other companies. Within a week, we were both notified by Lockheed to come in for an interview, after which we both received an offer. Lou accepted the offer and left FMC on short notice; I put in the standard, two-week notice. After joining Lou at Lockheed, he informed me that he had gotten an offer from one of the other companies at which we had applied. After having worked at Lockheed for two or three weeks, Lou stayed out for one week while he went to work for the other company; this to "test the waters" and make sure he was making the right move. Meanwhile, at Lockheed, I kept covering for Lou as best as I could. Well, Lou did like the other company, got an additional raise plus a promotion, and left Lockheed. He really was a dynamic kind of guy!

After three and a half years at Lockheed, I heard from Lou again; this time he was working at Dalmo Victor, this company being in Belmont, about 18 miles north of Sunnyvale. Lou was working as a Design Checker, which is one of the rungs in the ladder of Engineering Services that we in the business, aspired to reach. He called me at Lockheed, very enthusiastically, telling me that Dalmo Victor needed Design Checkers and that they were paying top money. I hesitated, lacking confidence, to which Lou, very kindly, said "I have the confidence in you, I worked with you for six years at FMC and I know you can do it." So, in 1965, I left Lockheed and joined Lou at Dalmo Victor as a Design Checker, and at quite a healthy raise. My job involved checking the design of gears, struts, and other mechanical parts for the Lunar Excursion Module (L.E.M.), which made it to the moon! I take great pride in that.

As a Design Checker, I regularly met with the Configuration Control Board to review the drawings for approval and to have them released for production. After I had been at Dalmo Victor for about three months, the CCB Manager went on vacation and asked me to sit in for him through that time. It was around this time that Lou, once again, saw a better move. Electromec, a job shop, was looking for designers to work under a contract for Bowing Aircraft, which paid a dollar more per hour than Dalmo Victor. An added feature was that Electromec was located in San Jose, in fact, across from, and just a short distance from FMC, where it had all begun for me.

Lou and I sent our resumes to Electromec and this time, I was made an offer, and for some reason, Lou was not. The contract at Electromec, actually turned out to be with IBM, whose headquarters was very close to our new house on Drifter. Although we worked "in house" at Electromec; the contract with IBM lasted more than six years. By this time, Gloria and I could afford "his" and "hers" vehicles. As happy and proud as I was of my little family while living at the Coyote house, my life was enriched ten-fold while living at the Drifter house; It was here that Bob and Ruby went through grade school as well as through high school. Gloria and I were very involved with their school activities as well as with their respective extra-curricular activities. Mainly, our time was more taken up by Bob's, which were Little League, Pal football, Cub Scouts and later, high school football. Through these activities, I was involved as a Little League coach as well as the director of the "C" league, while Gloria was very involved with bringing refreshments to the team, helping me with scheduling, and contacting team player's parents. She also helped me with getting equipment to the practices and to the games.

In Pal Football, Gloria was the League Secretary while I was asked to do the yearbook and help with fund-raising events. Getting my son to practices along with some of his teammates was a self-imposed task. Through the Cub Scout year, I was Scout Master; Gloria was the Den Mother, with the meetings usually taking place at our house. She was also helpful with planning the events. Throughout all this, Ruby became a voracious reader. Either on her birthday or for Christmas, we would buy her a Walter Farley's book, based on the series, The Black Stallion. This first book, I had absorbed deeply, when Miss Button, my sixth grade teacher at Greenfield Elementary, read it to the class every Friday. During Bob's games, Ruby would be reading one of these books, or some other book that had to do with horses. When she was in the eighth grade, her class was asked to take a comprehensive test to see what course of study each student would best be suited for in high school; Ruby scored college-freshman level in English.

From the age of five, Ruby displayed a commitment to all

kinds of animals. While living at Drifter, besides the family dog, Prince, Ruby owned several cats, and her new dog, Gamby, who along with her books, was her companion, during Bob's sports activities. At some point in time, Ruby also owned a snake, mice, a rabbit and eventually, horses.

My own, deep impression with The Black Stallion book, prompted me to buy Ruby each one of Walter Farley's books on the Black Stallion series; I believe that she now owns the entire series, or close to it. As much as she loved all her animals, her greatest love was horses. While Ruby was in the third grade at Glider, and Bob was in the sixth grade, Bob came home one day after school quite chagrined. "Mom, tell Ruby to stop acting like a horse at school, it's very embarrassing." It seems that at recess, or at lunchtime, Ruby would lead a "herd" of her classmates, neighing and snorting while galloping around the schoolyard. It was at this time, also, that Bob asked us not to call him "Bobbie" anymore; could girls have been on the horizon?

Perhaps, because of having lived in tents, old barns and a garage, or perhaps because of the poverty I experienced as a child; perhaps that is why I strove to own properties. My real dream has always been to own a small ranch with a few farm animals and a big "old" barn, where the grandkids can enjoy sleepovers on family visits. In any case, with Ruby's penchant for a horse, I started looking for a third property. To my surprise, I found an older country house on a three-quarter acre lot. It was located at 1145 Viewpoint Lane in Almaden Valley, which was predominantly horse country. The most pleasant surprise was that the property was selling for less than $40,000, which, less than ten years later, we sold for $145,000. Once again, we refinanced our Coyote Road house for the down payment, and now we owned three properties. These real estate dealings didn't bother me at all. In fact, I thought this to be very practical; I was too dumb and blind to realize the effect this was having on Gloria.

For Ruby's tenth birthday, we "surprised" her with a three-year old Morgan colt, Beau Brandon. While working at ESL in 1971, a fellow co-worker, Floyd Mansker happened to own Morgan show horses, and it was through him that we bought Beau. While Ruby's birthday activities were going on, Bob and I drove to Viewpoint to bring Beau. I had rented a horse trailer earlier in the day and had also bought a red horse blanket and a matching, red lead rope so that Beau would look his best. Amazingly, Beau was a very gentle colt; he must have been well trained before we got him; he walked into, and out of the trailer very easily.

Back at the house, the kids were playing in the backyard, and I parked on the Cozy Street side of the house. As quietly as we could, Bob and I walked Beau around the front, and through the far side of the house. Ruby was ecstatic! Without hesitation, she ran up to the colt, and gave him a big hug. I helped her up on Beau's back, and walked him around the backyard by his brand new lead rope.

Starting with Beau, we were later to have three more Morgan horses, one being a beautiful mare we bought for Beau, Easter's Wind Song. The other two were the result of breeding these two. Also, through this period of time, I was to learn a lot about horse. I learned "conformation," "withers", "forelock" and one term that shocked me because it came from my teenage daughter, was "teats." I also learned from Ruby about proper horse diet, horse training and shoeing, and most importantly, horse breeding; Gloria and I learned the cost of owning horses…all on our own.

We lived at the Viewpoint Lane house for one year while we rented out the Drifter house. We wanted to "feel" out country living. Right away, I started the very difficult task of clearing the lower part of the property, the little house being on the upper part. The ground was very rocky which made the task very difficult. Once that was done, I built a corral for Beau, and adjacent to it, I built a two-horse stall. Before we bought Beau, we had bought Ruby a quarter-pony, Sam, which was not too small, yet not too big for her to enjoy. This horse was a little frisky but Ruby rode him well and even managed to train him to jump over obstacles she set up. There were times when Ruby had trouble with Sam. In fact, when we were showing it to a prospective buyer, Sam went into a "rodeo" fit and almost bucked Ruby off. She hung on, but needless to say, the man took his young daughter by the hand and cordially thanked us and left. Eventually, we did sell Sam and it was a sad day for us, but especially sad for Ruby. To make matters worse, as we watched Sam being driven up Viewpoint, he turned his head, looking back at us. I will never forget that moment, nor, certainly, will Ruby.

After the year was over, we moved back to our Drifter house and rented the little country house with the condition that we keep the horses there. At this time, I was working at Measurex Corporation, where I was introduced into the Management arena; I became the Drafting Supervisor for the Drafting Department. Every day, after work, I drove over to Viewpoint to feed the horses. On weekends, Ruby would ride Beau and also train him how to "park," which is a stance show horses take when being shown. Not long after we had bought Easter's Wind Song, Ruby read up on the breeding process, which is, firstly, dependent on the mare being in "season," another word making its way into my horse "learning." I also learned that the mare was in season for a few days and that we were to breed her each of these days, to increase the chance of conception.

With Ruby's directions, we proceeded to breed Windy, as I called the mare. First, she had me put two tires on the outside railing of the corral, this to protect Windy, in case Beau got overly anxious. She then proceeded to wrap Windy's tail, here again to protect the mare. The horsetail hairs are like stands of copper wire, and wrapping helps prevent any injury during the breeding. Once we were all set, Ruby went into the corral, from where she held Windy with her lead rope. I, on the other hand, held Beau at bay with his lead rope, which was not easy, as I felt the enormous power of a stallion near a mare in season. Under normal conditions, Beau was exceptionally gentle. This being the first time for all concerned made the task somewhat awkward and more difficult then it needed to be.

From the very first breeding, Ruby kept a ledger throughout the gestation period. A week before the due date, she began insisting that I take her over to Viewpoint so that she could spend the night in the stall, and witness the birth. This, I resisted. I kept telling her to wait a few more days. I actually did not want her to spend the night out there; it was still out in a rural area and there were no streetlights. A few days later, I couldn't put her off anymore; she was very concerned, so I relented. Ruby took her dog Gamby, a portable radio, a flashlight, some bedding and some snacks with her. On one end of the stall, I put a four-by-four sheet of plywood as a lean-to. When everything was all set, I left, still quite concerned.

Very early the next morning, I drove over to check on Ruby before I went to work. As soon as I stepped in front of the stall, Ruby came out, sleep on her face, and said "Daddy! You're a grandpa!" I peeked inside the stall, and there was this long-legged, beautiful filly, standing on wobbly legs. I went in the stall and picked the filly up in my arms, something I had always though of doing. I carried her outside, with Windy following close by, and as soon as I put the filly down, she took off like a bullet, kicking and bucking, acting as if she was a "real" horse. Windy cantered over and directed the filly back. Shortly after the filly's birth, Ruby named her Leia.

When Leia was at the tender age of four months, Ruby showed her at the Santa Clara County Fair through her 4H Club; this little filly took the blue ribbon in her breed, and was selected as the Grand Champion between two other breeds! To say that we were proud is an understatement; we were flabbergasted! I remember having taken time off work to see this show, but Ruby insists that it was a later showing I had gone to, when Leia was a year old. Leia grew up to be very much like a pet dog in her relationship with us. I feel that this was so because of Ruby having been in the stall when Leia was born, and possibly, also because of my picking her up, right out of the chute, so-to-speak. The principal factor, I believe, is the fact that Ruby bestows so much attention, love and affection on all her pets.

One day, at the Palm Ave. property, I was working under my car in the garage, when I heard Leia's hooves approaching. Then, as she stepped into the garage, her hoof steps became more pronounced and Leia walked right up to my car, looked under it, and curiously checked it out. I had no concern that she might step on me, but I did "shoo" her away. Another antic of hers was to walk up the steps onto the deck outside the family room, where she would peek inside and basically, just loiter there for a while. One early afternoon, I had come home from work a little tipsy after a department picnic. I was very hungry when I got home and immediately threw a steak in a frying pan. I thought to lie down for a few minutes while the steak was frying, planning to check on it in a few minutes. Awakening twenty-five minutes later, I found the entire house filled with smoke! Quickly turning the burner off and removing the frying pan, I immediately went about opening every door and every window in the house. I also turned the air conditioner on; I did not want my wife to see, or smell, in this case, any evidence of my stupid mistake. Once the smoke dissipated, I went back to the bedroom and took a little nap. When I awoke, as I was walking past the family room, there was Leia and her younger sister, Jackie, loitering inside the family room! One was sniffing at the TV set while the other one was checking out a fake tree, in the corner of the room. They had both climbed up onto the deck and walked right in, through the open doors.

Through high school, Ruby was very involved with her horses, even taking Leia into one of her classrooms at Santa Teresa for a "show and tell" assignment; I still find it hard to believe the school allowed this. Bob, on the other hand, was busy playing football at Santa Teresa, and socializing with his buddies, and enjoying his new Toyota pickup. Eventually, I became concerned about one of his evening activities with his buddies, and finally

166

confronted him on this. Once a week, he and his friends would go to the "Mansion." He would either go meet his friends there, or they would come over and pick him up." Bob, what goes on at this 'Mansion' you guys hang around." "Dad," he replied, "you should come by sometime, several parents do. I'm sure you'd like it." It turned out that one of the high school coaches held bible study once a week, at this place, and this is where my son and his buddies were "hanging" out.

Among his buddies, was a young man by the name of Dave Jacobs. Unfortunately, during their sophomore year, Dave's parents were getting divorced and both moving out of San Jose. Dave didn't want to go to a new school, having to leave his friends and sweetheart behind. Bob asked if we could have Dave live with us through his last two years at Santa Teresa. We accepted Dave into our family and at some point in time he was calling Gloria "mom." For some reason, he always called me "Mr. Lara." Dave did graduate from Santa Teresa along with his friends and later married his childhood sweetheart. A twist to this is that Dave became a Pastor, having his own congregation, here in the Almaden Valley. It was he, who performed the wedding ceremony for our daughter, Ruby.

From the time we got Beau, I was spending a lot of time with Ruby; I was living my childhood dream, vicariously, through her. The financial pressure and my inattentiveness, not to mention my insensitivity, were taking a toll on Gloria. I was so blind-in-love with her, and so proud of my son and daughter, that I was blindly ignoring Gloria's place in the family charter; I was not giving her the credit she deserved for her unselfish contribution in giving our children a much better life than the one she and I had.

The final straw came after I talked Gloria into buying our "dream" house, a brand new custom home on two and one- half acres. The house was 3680 square feet, had five bedrooms, three full baths, an indoor laundry room, and a three-car garage. The place was also perfect for keeping horses, which was the major factor, as we now had three horses. The place also had white-railed fencing surrounding the perimeter of the property, with a circular driveway with an eight foot gate at each end. One added feature of this property, and which came as a 'bonus", was that it had a well. This was part of the dream; I would lift the cover off and drop small rocks down the well. There's something about that sound, similar, in emotion, as the sound of a train, somewhere in the distance.

In order to buy this house, we had to liquidate the other two rentals, as well as the Drifter house, which was painful, as we all considered the Drifter house our home; Bob and Ruby had lived out their childhood and teen years at this house; this may have been the final blow to Gloria, as she, more than any of us, considered the Drifter house to be home.

The move from the Viewpoint house was difficult and it took its toll on all of us. I have never believed in hiring a moving company; it is unnecessarily too expensive. We loaded the Toyota pickup and the family car and made several trips. When it came time to move the horses, I rented a two-horse trailer and took Windy and Leia; Ruby chose to ride Beau, while the rest of us took care of the move and the unpacking. The distance from Viewpoint to the new house, on Palm Avenue, is about ten miles, this, through hilly, country roads. The route Ruby took was about a quarter of a mile west of Viewpoint, towards Old Almaden. To the left, at this point, she rode south along McKean Road, which is all rolling hills and open country. Riding along Calero Reservoir a few miles down McKean, took Ruby to Bailey Avenue, which was the worst part of the ride, as it is through the highest, most winding, and narrowest road on the route.

Meanwhile, at the new place, Bob and I had put Windy and Leia away and brought in our house goods, while Gloria was unpacking and putting things away. By this time, it was getting dark and a light rain had started. We were getting concerned for Ruby, so it was decided that I backtrack and go find out where she was at that point. Before I took off, we saw headlights approaching the house. I went out to greet the strangers, who turned out to be an older couple. They informed us that they had seen Ruby, and had asked her if she needed help. Ruby asked them if they would please stop by the house and tell us that she was okay. We were very grateful to these strangers for their kind deed; it put us at ease knowing Ruby was okay, and close-by. Ruby got home within a half-hour after the strangers left. She was a little wet and very tired; she had ridden her stallion, Beau, a long distance through hilly country, in the rain, and with darkness approaching.

One of the first things I went about doing on the new place, was to put up a fence across the property on either side of the house, at the back. Behind this fence, which pretty much divided the property in half, I built a corral for Beau and left Leia and windy to roam free. At the front of the property, I decided to have a pump installed in the well, from which I proceeded to install a sprinkler system. The front portion of the property was approximately a half-acre and since there was a circular driveway, I had to trench the driveway at both sides of the yard.

This experience took place while I was working at a very small company, Braegan Corporation in Milpitas, California as a working Supervisor. The place was so small, I only had two drafters, and two ladies working the documentation section. Among the small circle of employees, there was one fellow, Jerry, who became a close friend. He and I, my small group and a few other employees would go out for pizza once a week, while Jerry and I would usually take our lunch and eat out somewhere, almost every day. Jerry was very well liked throughout the company. One of the ladies in Document Control was especially attentive to him. She was older than Jerry and was like a mother hen to him, simply caring for his well being. Jerry was the custodian and general handyman and was very popular throughout the company because of his personality and principally, because he was so unpretentious; he was the real deal.

At some point, a new employee was hired. She was an

attractive young lady who was to be our Lobby Receptionist. Although she was married, this pretty lady infatuated Jerry. I was not aware to what extent, until later that summer when Jerry offered to come and help me with the sprinkler system installation. I welcomed his offer, as the job was a bit much for one man. On that particular Saturday, Jerry was to come over early morning before it got too hot. I was up very early and was out trenching for a couple of hours before Jerry showed up.

He drove onto the driveway and as soon as he got out and started walking towards me, I could see that he was in bad shape; he had been out drinking and didn't look well at all. I went in the house and brought out two beers and we sat under the shade of a walnut tree; he opened up to me, stating that he had "really blown it' the night before.

Apparently, again unknown to me, Jerry had found out that this lady he liked, was working part-time in the evenings as a waitress, this at a restaurant-bar just across the freeway from Bragen Corporation. He had been stopping by for some time to see her and talk with her. Jerry told me that Friday evening he had gone over to see the girl and in the course of the evening, he had a few drinks too many and his conduct had offended the girl. When he finished telling me his story, he still offered to help me but he was in no shape to be digging trenches out in the heat. I thanked him and told him that it was too hot and that I was going to quit myself and continue in the evening. I recommended that he go home and sleep it off. With all due respect to some of my friends, under the same circumstances, I'm sure they would have called and either told me what had happened and that they just couldn't make it, or else come up with an excuse; Jerry, in spite of his condition, drove from Milpitas all the way to south San Jose to help me and I know now, that he needed someone to talk to and he knew he could talk to me.

Monday morning, I was at work very early. My boss was already in and rather than his usual "good morning" greeting, he called me into his office, a somber look on his face. "Jerry's dead." He said. I cannot tell you how stunned I by this enormous blow! I had just seen Jerry over the weekend and could not have realized the extent of his emotional state. When his "surrogate" mom came in, I gave the bad news and at first she thought I was kidding, but when she saw the pain in my face, she broke down and cried. That whole week and for some time after, the mood at work seemed to be cold and everything seemed to go in slow motion.

We were to find out that Jerry had gone back to the restaurant to try to talk to the girl once more, but things only got worse. As far as the girl was concerned, Jerry got out of hand and the matter turned ugly. Feeling rejected, Jerry said some things that offended the girl, and which he later regretted; but in any case, Jerry left in anger. Making his way to his pickup, Jerry was distraught and in this emotional state, got into the pickup and proceeded to ram the girl's parked car more than once. He told me he did it twice and as he drove home, the anger subsided and even in his drunken state, he realized what he had done and felt extremely guilty, stupid and very remorseful.

Sunday morning, the police came to where Jerry was living and found the obvious evidence on his pickup. They knocked on the door but got no response. The landlord was asked to open the door and the police found Jerry dead in his bed. That night, Jerry had showered, made sure his dog had food and water, got dressed for bed, and shot himself. This was such a tragic ending, and so undeservingly, for such a young person.

I eventually finished the sprinkler system through that summer and each day, as I worked, I thought of Jerry and his offer to help when he himself needed my help but I couldn't have known just how much.

Gloria and I went on about the business of settling down in our brand new "dream" house while Bob and Ruby were attending college. While Gloria was pleased with the house, she was also very concerned with our new financial burden. We now had a huge mortgage while putting Bob and Ruby through college; we also had three horses to maintain; all of this was quite a financial stretch. Fully aware of the "stretch", I was confident that we would make it; and looking back now, I know we would have.

Unfortunately, within a few years after living in the "dream house," I was rudely awakened from the dream. The financial stress, coupled with my indifference and insensitivity to her feelings, were just too much for Gloria. Although I felt I was doing right for our financial future, I had not taken the time to communicate this to her; I'm a nice guy, a good friend and a very good father, I was just not a good husband. When Gloria brought up the subject of divorce, call it hurt or pride, I went along with it. I remember thinking " I don't want her to be married to me if she isn't happy with me." I wish I had thought to explore the why and the how, instead of giving in to foolish pride.

One weekend, while Bob and Ruby were home, he from work and Ruby on a school break, Gloria asked that we all sit down and discuss the situation. She was the only one who spoke, stating her case, all of which was true, and then she asked if we had anything to say. I wish my son or my daughter had spoken their mind, mainly that Gloria and I not divorce. More painful than that, I wish I had spoken up against the divorce; in the back of my stupid mind, I feel that Gloria may have hoped that I talk her out of it. But, nothing was said from the three of us, and the pain and the pride won out.

What I had always considered to be a perfect marriage, and certainly, an amazing family, came to an end. For me, from that moment I got in step with Gloria in front of the freshman wing in 1953, through our thirty-two years together; for me, my life had been picture perfect, truly a wonderful life. I was not alone; all our friends and relatives were in disbelief when word got out about our divorce. One beautiful moment did come out of our divorce, if such is possible during such a painful step in life. This moment came out when my mother-in-law, Terry, said, "Rudy, this divorce is not going to make any difference; you will always be part of the family." Pain? I was not expecting nor prepared for the pain that was to follow.

With Bob and Ruby away, Gloria and I were alone in this big house; she stayed in the master bedroom, while I stayed in the guest room, these two rooms being at opposite ends of house. Initially, we were still riding to work together; she would drop me off in Fremont, and continue on to Sunnyvale. Very quickly, this became strenuous, both physically and emotionally for the two of us. Eventually, it became too awkward, and I started taking the bus to work. This was quite a painful experience in itself, since it required transferring busses four times, taking me two hours to get to work. On the other hand, this gave me time to reflect on my mistakes, and to feel sorry for myself. One very painful experience, while taking the bus, was when I "lost" an umbrella that had been a recent father's day present from my son.

Not long into our separation, Gloria was too uncomfortable having me at home, this, even though we hardly saw each. I tried to reason with her that financially, it was impractical for me to move, in addition to which, I was gone to work before she got up. She was adamant that I move out. I rented a room at a mobile home park from a very kind, elderly lady. The night I moved was a very rainy night. My son, Bob had driven me to the trailer park and on his way back home, he was going to stop at his grandmother's house. Later that night, the landlady knocked on my door and told me I had a phone call; it was my son and he had gotten into an accident. Bob was all right, but the car received extensive damage. This was the first time, throughout the separation, that I broke down and cried; I felt very low, and very guilty!

There was another tenant at the mobile home, a well-educated gentleman, who unfortunately, had a drinking problem. He and I would discuss history and other subjects of interest in the evenings. We shared the same interest in the Native Americans and he was well versed on the subject. But on most Friday nights, he changed into an entirely different person; he would come in very drunk and voice a very low opinion about Mexicans. At first, I would tolerate it, in light of his drunken stupor, but eventually, it became unbearable and I felt that I might have to belt him one; that would have been an extreme, for me.

I moved back home, much to Gloria's disapproval, so strongly, in fact, that she moved out. This was the beginning of a very painful spell for me. Though it was awkward being in the same house, at least we were together; at least I knew she was there. Her leaving was the beginning of final closure, which was very difficult for me to deal with. I would come home from work, feed the horses and bring our dog, Tasha in the house, just to "feel" part of my family still with me. Through this period, the tears came easier, and in greater quantities.

While Gloria and I were going through the divorce, I had started working at Lam Research supervising an Engineering Services department. On the same day I was going through the company orientation, this lady was also going through the process. I've always had a difficult time adjusting to a new company, and meeting new people; this lady, having the orientation in common with me, made me feel comfortable, like already knowing someone at work. Although she worked in a different department and in a different building, we would greet each other each time our paths crossed. At company meetings or other functions, I sought her out, because she was someone I "knew" and this brought me some comfort. Meanwhile, the full impact of having lost Gloria was weighing heavily on me. When the final papers came, it all seemed unreal. I began a campaign to try and get her back by calling her and asking that we meet, just to talk. During the separation, she had told me that we could still be friends and that I could call her whenever I needed to talk. I didn't just want to talk; I wanted her back. I asked her to give us another chance. At first she would tell me that it was too soon, that she needed time. I eased back on my calling, which was very difficult, but when I did call again, she still said that it was too soon and that I should meet "other people."

Eventually, we sold our "dream house" and I moved further south, on Day Road, in Gilroy. The place I was renting was a one-bedroom, one-bath, "foreman's" quarters. The property around it, a few hundred acres, had once been a cattle ranch, and on the property, there were corrals for the horse, which is the reason why I moved there. Very soon, things got even more painful; we had to get rid of the horses. We sold Easter's Windsong, if I remember correctly, for $400 dollars; originally, we had paid $2500 dollars for her. Beau was given to a family that was leasing part of the property, at the time, running a small herd of cattle. Beau was easy to ride, and very gentle; the man, Mr. Gonzalez, liked Beau very much and used to ride Beau with our permission, while herding cattle. As our family situation got beyond our control, we let Mr. Gonzalez have Beau. Ruby did keep Leia and her sister, Jackie, both being kept at Ruby's ex-in-law's mini-ranch.

Almost a year went by and I still had hopes that Gloria would come back; I felt very strongly that we belonged together. Meanwhile, my lady friend and I were spending more time together, but strictly platonic, as I was not ready to date. For one thing, having met Gloria when she was fourteen and I seventeen, and now, here I was at age 50; I had no clue about the dating scene in the eighties. Another thing was the fact that, if I dated another girl, I would feel guilty, as if I were cheating, and that I would lose any chance of getting Gloria back. Eventually, Gloria was to tell me, "It's too late. You should find someone else and make a new life for yourself." Well, that was the final blow, and I had to accept it; it was actually a form of relief, perhaps now I would not feel guilty dating. I still didn't go out and start dating for some time; I didn't know how. The social scene between the fifties and the eighties were worlds apart.

A year after having met my lady friend at work, we happened to cross paths between buildings. We stopped to talk and she came right out and said, "You know, you've known me for a year now, and you haven't asked me out once." I made a lame excuse that my car wasn't in great shape and I was embarrassed. This was actually true; I was driving an older Volkswagen that I had bought from a fellow employee. The car would pop loudly each time I started it, this followed by billowing smoke. The hood was tied down with wire, as it had popped open one day while driving down Altamont Pass, a hilly, and very windy section between Tracy and Livermore. This lady, offered to drive her car. So on our first date, I drove my car to her house and from there we took hers. This was the beginning of a relationship that did not work out; I was too far removed from the current social crowd and I still couldn't get Gloria out of my mind.

Eddie Payne, my high school buddy, was back in the scene; he too, was divorced…three times! This is the period when our friendship became as close to family as is possible. His family "adopted" me as a member to the extent that Eddie's youngest nephews and nieces called me "uncle" Rudy. Sometimes, when we went over to his sister, Eva's house, as soon as we approached, the kids would come out, run past Eddie, happily greeting me. This would irk Eddie, but the kids had good reason; Eddie was inevitably, pretty rough on them, verbally, and physically, although, playfully. For the next few years, as a "member" of the family, I would spend holidays with them, as well as birthdays. Two family members asked me to be Godfather to their respective child; Eddie and I were like brothers by this time. At family gatherings, his dear mother would say to me, "Rudy, please look after Eddie." She had reason to be concerned; Eddie has had quite a life! Which reminds me of one incident even he, still tells friends. On an outing one day we were passing by a bar/pool hall he frequented. He said, "Lets stop by for one!" "Eddie, it's only ten-thirty in the morning!" "Just one," he repeated. We went in and ordered our beers and while he went and talked to his friend, who was shooting pool, I sat at the bar. Before I was halfway through my beer, Eddied came by and asked, "Ready for another one?" Well, I reminded him that we had agreed on "just one" and he knows I'm a stickler for a man keeping his word. He won't let me forget that incident.

From the mid-eighties on, the semiconductor industry began a spiral downturn; along with many other companies in Silicon Valley, Lam Research was affected. Initially, there was a small layoff through which my department was not affected. Later in the year, another layoff, this one bigger than the first, took place. Through this one, once again, my department was not affected. Then came the big one: close to 30% of the company force was laid off; this time several employees from my department were affected...including me. It's somewhat humorous to me that, upon handing me my last check, my boss said, "The problem with you, Ruben, is that you're too nice." Oh well, I couple this with what I consider as the highest, professional compliment I ever got throughout my entire career.

When I was hired to manage the Drafting/Design group at Lam Research, I wasn't told that the department was known as the "sweat hogs," throughout the company. A few "bad apples" had a tendency to leave early for lunch and come back late. There was one fellow that was on probation on a drug-related charge. This one also had the tendency to tilt his drafting board up about 30 degrees and either take a nap, or read the paper... during working hours, of course. These issues came to a halt upon my arrival, simply because as their new boss, they didn't yet know how to read me. I am a nice guy; they saw this, but they also saw my demeanor for professionalism.

The only real encounter I had was with one of my Design Checkers and a young Drafter. One Friday I noticed the two had left about 11:30. I inquired as to their whereabouts and was told that they had left early to get to the bank; they also came back from lunch close to 1:00. When I asked for the timecards to be turned in, these two individuals had filled in a full eight hours on their respective time cards. I took these back and asked that they be corrected. The Design Checker did so without any problem, in fact he chuckled, knowing better. The younger one, the Drafter, came up to my desk and said, "I'm not changing my timecard." and walked away. I told him, "It's up to you, but I'm not going to sign it, and personnel won't issue a check until I do." He changed his time card. I didn't have any other problems with my group; in fact, we got along fine.

Several months after having been hired, I went over to Manufacturing, which was in another building, to drop off a documentation package. As I stepped into the lobby, I heard the familiar voice of the CEO of the company. "Ruben!" he called out. "Stop by on your way back." I was a little apprehensive and curious, as to what the CEO of the company would want to see me about. On the way back, I peeked in his office and was asked to come in. What he had to say was the following: "I've heard it from Department Managers throughout the company, and I thought I'd tell you myself. I want to thank you personally for an amazing job you've done with your department." For me, that was the epitome of a professional compliment. The Kid From Del Rio had gone up through the ranks in Engineering Services, and this, without the benefit of a college degree, just a solid, educational grounding in Del Rio… with a little help from my friends.

It took me several years to blend into a new social life. I was now hanging out with my buddy Eddie and a group of old James Lick pals. I was now feeling comfortable going out and enjoying it. One of our favorite hangouts was a country-western dancing place named "Cow Town." Here, we met several people with whom we shared personal similarities. A lot of single and divorced ladies showed up every Friday. Thursdays happened to be "Ladies Night," which included a free spaghetti and garlic bread dinner; this was perfect for us bachelor guys! At this time, I was working at By Video, in Sunnyvale. This small company happened to be just a few blocks from ESL, a former employer of mine. ESL was the company that made headline news when a rejected "lover," methodically walked in and gunned down several employees. We, at By Video, were listening on the radio as this was going on; the area around us was blocked off for hours. While at By Video, I worked for a close friend and former colleague at Measurex, Denny Taketa. Denny was supervising a Drafting/Documentation group that included one girl handling the documentation, while another fellow, Dennis, and I took care of the design and drafting. The company, as a whole, was very small and made for close friendships and a good work environment. It was here that I met Barbara, a woman whom I took out once. She and another woman, Audrey, alternated in manning the lobby, and as it turned out, Audrey is the one I wound up dating for quite some time. Barbara, who is Mexican-American, and quite younger than I, happened to be the niece of Manuel Silva, who is married to the oldest of my five, girl cousins, Olivia. While I had known Manuel for many years through the family, I hadn't met Barbara until my stint at By Video.

For our "date," I took Barbara on a tailgate picnic to a football game in San Francisco. She had a boyfriend at the time, and in fact, Barbara told me that he had dropped her off where she and I had decided to meet. Our date was strictly platonic, with all concerned, fully aware of this. Barbara brought up the subject of a divorcee friend of hers, and thought that I might be interested in meeting her. Barbara farther told me that she had brought up the subject with her friend and that, she too, had expressed interested in meeting me. This close friend of Barbara's was described to me as being very nice and attractive. The "very nice" has always fit my pistol a little better than the "attractive" side of a woman; this lady was both.

With Barbara as a go-between, I was invited to a Halloween party at this woman's house; this would have been in1987. For morale support, I took Eddie and another friend, Tim Mumson, along. Eddie went dressed as a bad Mexican "bandit." I forget what Tim wore; I went as Zorro. I had no way of knowing that it was Barbara's friend who answered the door upon our arrival. After introducing ourselves, she led us straight to the decorated garage, where the rest of her guest had congregated. With the place quite crowded, the three of us sat with our backs to the garage door. After everyone had eaten, the lights were dimmed and the dancing music began. This "friend" that Barbara wanted me to meet came up and asked me to dance. She was attractive; she had the smiling eyes and the sweet smiling lips of a Linda Ronstadt.   Going through the informal introductions as we danced, we got to the part concerning each other's point of origin. When I told her that I was from Del Rio, Texas, she looked up at me and said, "My family's from Del Rio." I actually wasn't too surprised, as there are many families from Del Rio, here in San Jose. But I was very surprised when she told me who her family was. When she told me that it was her mother, who was from Del Rio, and that her grandfather was from Rocksprings, Texas, I stopped dancing. I asked her what her grandfather's name was and when she said Jose Mendez, I stopped cold! With an instant surge of love and pride, I put my arms around this beautiful stranger and lifting her up while twirling her around, I exclaimed, "He's my uncle, my mother's brother." Well, that ended any possibility for a blooming romance, but I had found a beautiful cousin that otherwise, I may have never known. That's the way love goes.

Soon after this "blind date" with my cousin, whose name is Elida, Audrey and I started going out to lunch frequently and eventually, became "an item," throughout the company. Audrey was a gorgeous young lady, very young; in fact, she was twenty-two years my junior. Besides a beautiful face (and figure), Audrey had this huge mane of red hair, much like Reba McKentire used to have. One day, early on into our "relationship," we were heading out to lunch when Audrey asked me if I minded stopping by her house first; she wanted to pick up some papers that she had forgotten that morning.

When we arrived at her place, we went in and she took me on a casual tour, explaining that she and another woman had bought the house. Going into the kitchen, she asked me if I wanted a drink and I nodded yes. With our drinks in our hands, Audrey then took me out to see the backyard, which was beautifully landscaped, with several mature fruit trees with a path leading between them. Enjoying this serene backyard, we finished our drinks and headed back in the house where she picked up the papers she had forgotten, and we went off to lunch.

Back at work, I related my adventure to the guys and of course, they assumed other things to have happened. This naïve mind of mine, was a little concerned; here I was in a perfectly, suitable situation to have at least stolen a kiss, the setting being perfect, and, after all, it's the American way...universal, actually. Well, the next time Audrey needed to stop by her house before we went to lunch, as soon as she had poured us a short drink, I took her by the hand and led out the kitchen to the backyard, where I took her in my arms and gave her a big kiss. Taking her by the arm once more, I led her back in the house and right there, in the kitchen, I planted another kiss on her sweet lips. "I should have done this the first time we were here," I told her. "It's been bothering me that I didn't." She just looked up at me with these beautiful eyes and nodded okay, and we left for lunch.

For almost two years, Audrey and I attended events together. First, company picnics, then the company Christmas party and later on, Cow Town. As it was, we were both pretty much equally awkward on the dancing floor, so we decided to take dancing lessons at a small dance studio in Willow Glen. We did this for several months but to no avail; we nicked-named each other "Twinkle Toes." Our social outings included barbecues at a friend's house; I even wound up taking her to a Del Rio dance, where she was undoubtebly, the only white person. That not withstanding, she stood out with that huge, full, red mane of hers. Some time, in the early part of 1988, Audrey and her partner sold the house in Sunnyvale and bought another house on her own; this turned out to be a financial disaster, and I believe she lost, or sold this house. I heard, a couple years later, that she had gotten married and had moved to New York. Wherever she is, I hope she's doing fine and has learned to dance, just as I haven't.

By now, Cow Town was a regular hangout for the little gang of mine. There were four of us that usually hung out together, but we got to know several other people at Cow Town who became part of our group. By this time, Eddie had been divorced four times; the rest of us were still single. This was the year that I felt I was completely healed from my divorce; it had taken a few years. Among our group of friends, we shared many barbecues and holiday celebrations at one, or the other's house. Socially, It was a robust and happy period; but then, a weird thing happened. On one of our nights at Cow Town, I was heading to the bar to order a beer and got a shock to my system. I was sure that I had seen Gloria on the dance floor! After all this time, after all the pain, those old feelings came roaring back, the initial feeling of guilt, that feeling of having been "caught." I hurried back to the group and got Eddie's attention. "I just saw Gloria!" He too, found it hard to believe, so we made our way towards the dance floor, looking for her. Sure enough, there she was, or so we thought. She looked so much like her, but still, neither one of us was quite sure. We took another look and walked away, still wondering.

Quite moved by this experience, I went back and stood by the dancing floor to get a closer look. Eventually, Eddie and I determined that it wasn't Gloria. This woman looked so much like her that she could have been her twin. Eventually, I approached this look-alike and asked her to dance. From then on, for a few months, we began dating.

On one of the barbecues with my group of friends, this one having taken place at my house, I took a candid photo of my new date; it was a portrait shot with a telephoto lens, without her being aware I had taken it. Later that year, one of my friends from the group, Jorge Treviño and I, went on a trip through San Antonio, Galveston, and of course, Del Rio, which is also Jorge's hometown. I took Mary's picture with me to show it to my sister, Minnie. In Del Rio, I checked into a motel before I drove the rental car to my sister's house. Her house, at this time, was just across the street from the property our father had left us. On the very first lot, directly across from Minnie's house was the old Esquivel house. That old friend looked old, weathered and a little bent, but still standing. When I arrived at my sister's, she and a neighbor were in the backyard, visiting. After my sister introduced me to the lady, I took out my lady friend's photo and asked her, "Who's this?" Without hesitation, she replied, "Gloria." I explained what had transpired back in San Jose, and that this was someone I was dating. Very surprised at the likeness, she told me to go in the house and show the picture to my brother-in-law, Pablo (Beaver). He too, immediately thought the woman in the picture was Gloria.

My relationship with this new lady did not last very long, and shortly after having ended our relationship, I was back with my old group, as a "single" again. On one of these nights at Cow Town, I saw this beautiful, green-eyed woman. I was immediately impressed by her beauty and asked her to dance. The very first thing she said to me as we were dancing was, "I'm fifty years old." I don't know if this was plain openness, or if she was trying to let me know that she was no young girl to be fooled with. I took it to mean honesty, to which I replied, "I'm fifty-three." We exchanged names, at which time I found her name to be Judy. For the next few weeks, I looked forward to seeing her, and when she was not there, I pestered her girlfriends for her phone number, too no avail.

One night, close to closing time and as everyone was starting to leave, I asked Judy if she would stop by and have a cup of coffee with me. She was hesitant, but I convinced her. At the time, I was transporting a Columbian friend of Eddie's, whom Eddie had asked me to put up for a couple of days. Just for the record, typical of Eddie, my best buddy since high school, my "adopted" brother, was a scoundrel. All of us, his friends, his family, knew this only too well, but you can't help but like the guy; he ain't heavy, he's my brother. Some weeks before, Eddie had sold me on a story that his daughter was going to stay with him for a few days, and he didn't want his daughter feeling uncomfortable around this man. I was living alone in a four-bedroom house, so there was no problem in putting his friend up for a few days. Well, Eddie has a tendency to fib a little and the truth of the matter was that he just wanted to get rid of this man, who had been pawned on him by another friend of ours. Well, the Columbian we called Molacho (toothless), wound up staying a couple of months with me. He paid me some "rent" whenever he could, but left me with a long-distance phone bill of more than sixty dollars. Nevertheless, Judy agreed to meet me at a little hole-in-the-wall eatery called "Just Breakfast" that was not far from Cow Town. We had our cup of coffee and the meeting was very brief due to the fact that it was rather late, and I had Molacho with me.

I walked Judy to her car, while Molacho walked on ahead to my car, which was parked out on the street. For the record, once again, since I' am not a drinking man, to drown my sorrows after my divorce, I had bought myself a brand new, 1988 Mazda RX7, sports car. So, while Molacho went to the car, I took Judy in my arms and kissed her goodnight. From the following Friday night at Cow Town on, Judy and I became a twosome; just meeting at Cow Town for a couple of weeks, then started dating regularly. About that very first night we met at Cow Town, I kid Judy about her having roped me, and then hog-tied me so that I wouldn't run off. I still have the indelible, branding iron logo on this frail body of mine.

On August 19, 1990, we were married. The young man, who performed our wedding services, was no other than my son's high school friend, Dave Jacobs. Our wedding was simple, with the service being performed outdoors, on the beautiful gardens of Garden Alameda; the reception took place at Napredak Hall. Along with Judy's small family, some of her friends from KR Smith School were there. Judy has worked at this elementary school for the past 37 years, having known several of my nephews and nieces long before she and I met, and some of whom I had not yet met! My daughter and son were present, as were several of my former colleagues with whom I had worked at various companies. This time Eddie was my best man, and this time he brought his fifth wife, from whom he was to be divorced not too long thereafter.

Eddie cannot be pinned down; today, he makes his home in Modesto, where he lives with one of his daughters and son-in-law; he also lives, for short periods at a time, in Reno, with his sister Eva, with whom he lived in San Jose during the time I was "adopted" as "uncle" Rudy. Eddie also stays with a friend, here in San Jose, periodically, which is the only time our mutual buddy, Tony Barrera and I, get to see him.

Through the past fifteen years or so, Eddie and I have made several trips to Tombstone Arizona, where one of our best trips was during a Western Film Festival held there. Among the guests, all 50's TV stars, we got to meet Clint Walker of *Cheyenne Body* fame, Dale Robertson of *Tales of Wells Fargo*, Will Hutchins of *Sugar Foot* and Harry Carry Jr. who, as his father did, was featured in many John Wayne movies. Both Eddie and I share a similar interest in the southwest forties movies, and the fifties music. We make a nuisance of ourselves with our respective mates on these subjects. Invariably we get, "You guys are living in the past instead of the present!" Well, I don't particularly care how the present is going, and there will never be another time like the one we had in the forties.

Prior to my marriage, Eddie and I made several trips to Ensenada, a quaint and beautiful, seacoast Mexican town approximately seventy miles south of San Diego, in Baja California. We've been to Del Rio and San Antonio several times and one trip that we've planned for, several times, but have yet to fulfill, is a Southwest tour from California to Texas and heading northwest from San Antonio to Amarillo. From there, the plan is to spend a day or two in Taos New Mexico and then back to California with a few stops at selected points, such as the Grand Canyon, Las Vegas and Death Valley. Most likely, we would make another stop in Tombstone; this Wyatt Earp town has quite a pull on us. Unfortunately, Eddie has suffered from severe knee problems and each time we've had to forego our plans. Recently, he had one knee operated on and is slowly recovering. He tells me that the pain is so severe that he told the nurse to have his leg amputated, adding, "ll sign any papers!" Besides a low tolerance for pain, Eddie has an enormous sense of humor. Perhaps, like in the movie *The Bucket List*, we'll fulfill our plan yet.

Some of the excursions Eddie and I have been on took place after Judy and I were married. She is very understanding and is very aware of my nostalgic devotion to Del Rio, Texas. Judy is also a no-nonsense kind of woman. She has no false pretences and is the biggest sissy when it comes to patriotism... next ta me, pilgrim. We both share the same love for America in the forties and we put the American flag out everyday of the year. Judy also likes to frame and hang on the walls the Veteran's posters that come out every year. We also enjoy going to the Memorial Day Services every year. Judy is also a "neat freak." Before we were married, I had wall-hanging prints on the floor (but at least, they were leaning on the wall!) On the living room couch, I had a saddle that belonged to my son. That all changed after Judy invaded my bachelor's pad. So much, in fact, that some of my friends commented the house now looks like a model home. She is an excellent interior decorator and could be doing it professionally, but she has too many years invested at KR Smith School. It amazes me how much of a neat freak she is. Because of this, whenever I have a bowl of cereal or, especially, cookies, I make sure to pick up every little crumb, and would you believe it? She gets home and before long, she'll ask, "You had cookies in the family room, didn't you?" She will find the smallest, little piece of evidence, no matter how careful I am! Judy is also a hardworking Dodo head; before she leaves for work, on a washday, she'll say, "bring your white clothes to the washer." When she gets home, before going in he house, she turns the washer on, walks in, gets the cleaning stuff, and proceeds to clean both bathrooms! The only thing she asks me to do, during this chore, is to shake the bathroom rugs outside, to which I always exclaim, "I have to do everything, around here!" Afterwards, she'll ask, "What do you want for dinner?" I am one very fortunate man!

It's nice having been married in our middle-age years, our relationship is more solid in that, there is no room left for jealousy or insecurities; what you see, is what you get. Judy and I get along fine and we give each other plenty of space for our respective hobbies, hers being crafts, crochet, and cooking. The latter one, being one of complete compatibility, as one of my favorite hobbies is eating. Actually, one of the first things I told Judy was that as long we had eggs, potatoes, beans and a piece of steak now and again, she wouldn't have to worry about what to cook. An irony, concerning my marriage to Judy, is the fact that her first husband, George Snyder, was a fellow classmate of mine at James Lick! Judy was born in Port Angeles, Washington and was working in Seattle when she met George, who was stationed there, at the time. My hobbies have always been drawing and designing "gadgets," which my career was all about. I have an invention and have all the required drawings done in AutoCad and I have also written the patent application, but do not the funds for a prototype…maybe some day. I have also liked photography and gardening. My writing hobby came rather late in my life. Although I did very well in all my English courses, including Critical Thinking (English 1C), I never felt the "urge" to write. The urge to write hit me hard when, in 1977, George Lucas and Francis Ford Coppola gave us *American Graffiti*. I saw this movie seven times, and it not only took me back, emotionally, to my teenage years; it picked me up by the collar and the seat of my pants and placed me back to those years, a "Back To The Future " experience. This experience compelled me to write a sequel, which required that I learn screenplay writing. In the process of learning such, in a course I took at San Jose State University, we were assigned to write a half-hour documentary, which, I later developed into a short story; it is still "in process," and I hope to expand it into a novel. It's great to be retired and to have the freedom to pursue my writing. Judy allows me this "space" to write as well as for my other hobbies, as long as I'm on call for Wal-Mart, the Mall, or the grocery store. As to all our shopping tours, I'm the designated driver, even when we go to Almaden Lake for our daily walk.

Judy came into my life as a bundled package. At the time of our marriage, she had her two beautiful daughters Lisa, who is my son's age, and Lorie, who is a year and a half younger. At the time of our marriage, Lisa had an eight-year old daughter, Alma, whom she had adopted as a baby. Alma's biological parents were from San Salvador, and soon after Alma was born in 1980, Lisa and her husband adopted her. Alma's sister Sara, was born six years later. Lori, at this time, had a set of twins, Steven and Jaime, who were born less than a year before Judy and I wed. As of today, Alma has two daughters, Marisa and, Alisa, Marisa having been born with a medical condition that caused her to have seizures. As a result of the illness, she also has a speech impediment. Nevertheless, Marisa is a very happy and lovable child. Boy, howdy, can she walk through anything, or anyone, that gets in her way!

The very first time I saw the twins, Steve and Jamie, I named them Punk and Punkette. Alma's two daughters, Judy and I named Sissy and Mini-sissy. Unfortunately, and very painfully, we lost Steve recently, and our lives, understandably, have been much affected; he was only seventeen years old. Steve was a character, always "terrorizing" his sister with his antics, and similarly, his aunt, Lisa. One of the things I regret not having done with Steve, is letting him drive my 1957 Ford Fairlane 500, which he wanted to do. We talked about it, but it didn't happen; he was not of age. Every Christmas, for the past few years, we all gathered at our house and it became traditional to load everyone, and I mean from great-grand ma, Judy, to sisters Lisa and Lori, and all the kids, into the Ford Somehow, we would all bunch up in this fifties classic and drive to a part of our community, not far from our house, where every house and the respective front yards on the block, are lavishly lit, including all the trees along each street; this had become a family treat every Christmas.

From my side, Judy inherited a bundled package herself. This consisted of my son Bob and daughter Ruby. At the time, Ruby was married to Brian Moore. They gave Gloria and me our first grandchild, Jessica Lara Moore, who is nine and, now, my new "Tweekart." Bob and his wife, Lori, gave us two grandsons, Jake, six and Joshua, four. Judy and I kid about having Josh and Mini-sissy being turned loose in the house, at the same time; both are little bulldozers!

Lori, Judy's daughter, lives in Fremont, about twenty miles from San Jose, while Lisa lives within five miles from our house. On the other hand, my daughter, Ruby, lives in Sacramento, while Bob lives thirty miles farther north, in El Dorado Hills, about an hour away from Lake Tahoe. Judy's daughter, Lori, works in the Purchasing Department at a company named Harbor View, while Lisa has been working at Costco for several years, the store being very close from her home. Ruby followed her dream to work with animals, and has been working at the Sacramento Zoo as a Zoo Keeper for several years. Recently, she began tutoring math at Jessica's elementary school. Bob now works for Cisco, in the Marketing Department. He works from home, as do other employees, including his boss. Occasionally, Bob comes to San Jose for meetings at Cisco's Headquarters, and on such occasions, time permitting, we meet for lunch, or he stops by, on his way home.

In June of 1996, Judy and I went on vacation to her hometown, Port Angeles, Washington. It is beautiful country, no Del Rio, but I was impressed, nevertheless. With reference to Round Mountain in Del Rio, Judy would point to the Olympic National Park and comment, "Now, these, are mountains!" Judy and I went back to Port Angeles again in August of 2006. This time we went to spend time with Judy's childhood friends, Clare and Karen Winters, who had hit the state lottery a few years before, but have maintained their "down-home" personalities.

They still live in the same house they've lived in for many years. Ironically, the street the Winters live on, is named Winter Haven. We had found out that Karen has cancer and was undergoing chemotherapy. We were shocked at how much weight she had lost, but as I said, these friends have maintained the same warm personality, the same friendliness, and the same attitude, as when they were both working folk. We plan to go back to Port Angeles in August 2008 for Judy's fifty-year, high school reunion. Prior to that, in July, I hope to go to Del Rio for their fifty-two year reunion, God willing and financial circumstances prevailing.

In 2006, I received a form concerning an impending James Lick High, fifty-year reunion. The form asked for a 1956 photo and a current photo; it further asked that we list a few of our favorite memories of those four years at Lick. The heart of the form asked that we write a synopsis on our life, after Lick. I e-mailed my completed form to the reunion chairperson and asked if I could help in some capacity. The first meeting I attended was a blast for me! Although I hadn't known any of the committee members as close friends during our high school days, I remembered most of them; this alone, was very rewarding to me. The "capacity" for which I was volunteered, was based on my art background and my career in drafting. I was asked to design and publish a class book for the reunion attendees. While at James Lick, Eddie and I, with our years of Art classes always went "all out" in designing covers for our English class assignments. Fortunately, I do happen to enjoy designing. I used Adobe Photoshop and Adobe PageMaker in designing the class book. I had learned both of these programs during a fourteen-month long, Desktop Publishing program. This program was made possible through EDD, which paid for it during a lengthy, unemployment period.

The class book was well received by the Class of '56 attendees, but the icing on the cake came a little over a year later. While working on the class book, I researched archive photos of James Lick with the help of the school secretary,

Shari, who happened to be working that summer. She asked me to show her the class book when it was finished. Just recently, I went to James Lick to request a copy of my transcript and I had the opportunity to show Shari the class book. She was very impressed and kept exclaiming about it as she paged through it. Just then the Principal walked by and she showed him the book, and he too, was impressed. As he paged through it, the Principal came up with the idea that the book might be helpful reading material for the current student body. He pointed out that it would be beneficial for the students to get a glimpse of how the we dressed then, what some of our favorite memories were, and especially, what we had done with our lives "after" James Lick. To my surprise, he asked me to see if I could have thirty or thirty-five copies ordered, these to be used at James Lick. This was the highlight of all the nice compliments I had gotten on the class book! The school wound up ordering thirty copies, these to become a small part of the curriculum, within James Lick High!

Having retired in 2001 has given me the time to do things like writing and publishing the class book. I will continue to write, just for the love of it. I will continue to be involved with future high school reunions and look forward to the next one. I will also strive to go back and visit Del Rio, for as long as my health and finances allow.

I am so fortunate that Judy came along and has given me a second chance in life. Along with my own precious little family, her little family has become a major part in this second life. I thank Gloria for those wonderful, happy years she gave me, and I apologize for any unhappiness I caused her, throughout those years. I thank her dearly, for the two amazing children she gave me, both whom have turned out to be outstanding human beings. Most of all, I am so thankful for our grandchildren, Jessica, Jake and Josh; it is primarily for them, that I have written this book. I ask Bob and Ruby to chronicle their stories and add them to mine. I ask that Jessica, Jake and Josh make note of their childhood so that my great- grand children too, may share these. Similarly, I ask that all my nephews and nieces continue chronicling our ancestry.

So there it is, the end of my story, a story of a wonderful childhood through the forties, a story of my teenage years through the fifties, of family and of friends, the story of the Kid from Del Rio.

New baby, Robert with mom, Gloria.

Little Drummer Boy Bob's first Christmas at Coyote Road house.

The Kid from Del Rio with his new son, Robert

Bob, while shopping at Alpha Beta

Ruby, growing up

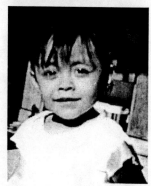

My little "Tweekart" Ruby

Gloria with Bob and Ruby at one of my football games with Club San Felipe.

Gloria, and my mother with Bob and Ruby at mother's house on Pickford Ave.

Bob with pet goat at Coyote Road house.

Young rebel guarding his sister, Ruby (Disneyland 1962)

Proud dad holding son and daughter

Such a cutie, that's my
daughter Ruby

My second little "Tweekart"
a Ruby look-alike Jessica
Lara Moore, (my very first
grandchild).

Jake and cousin
Jessica

School girl, granddaughter
Jessica

Jessica with Granopa at
Hoffman Park, Effie Yeau
Center in Carmichael, Califor-
nia (just north of Sacramento).

My sister Locha on a visit to her house in Modesto, California.

Ruby with Easter's Wind Song at Gilroy cattle ranch where we kept our stallion Beau Brandon and Leia, (Beau and Windsong's filly) I lived at this place for a while.

Wife Judy and the Kid somewhere on a week-end trip.

Son Robert with wife, Lori on a visit to my house here in San Jose. They live in El Dorado Hills, California, about 30 minutes from Sacramento.

Grown-up Ruby in a Little Sister calendar for Bob's fraternity at San Jose State University (although, Ruby was attending University of California at Davies at the time.

My buddy Eddie Payne and best man at my wedding to Judy, at Garden Alameda in San Jose.

I was into photography for many years, starting in the early 60's. This photo was taken by a collegue at FMC, who was a Senior Mechanical Designer and a professional photographer, as well.

Judy on an earlier backyard BBQ with grandchildren Steve, and twin sister, Jamie on either side and Alma, seated with great-granddaughter, Marisa.

Judy's grandchildren on an even earlier backyard BBQ. L. to R.: Sara, Steve, Alma, and Jamie.

Oh, youth! Where have you gone? An earlier photo (much earlier); I used to have black hair, then.

CHAPTER 14

THE BEGINNING

Herein, is the real beginning in the story of *The Kid From Del Rio* ...my ancestral heritage. Most of the following is on my paternal side, although I was able to find quite a bit of information on my maternal side. That portion that is on my paternal side, I owe to my grandaunt, Eloisa Hernandez Lara, from whose memoirs I discovered a wealth of information. I also learned that she had been married to my grandfather's brother, my grandfather being married to her sister, Mama Faustina, which is how we addressed our grandmother. This information was of great interest to me, a very rich discovery.

My paternal grandfather, Hilario Lara, was born in El Paso County in 1869 (probably in Presidio Texas) and died in Del Rio on September 21, 1938. My mother was to tell me in later years, that whenever my grandfather picked me up, I would play with his hair; at least I got to share two years of my life with him, although, at that age, I could not have retained that memory.

My paternal great-grandfather, Blas Lara, was born in Mexico in 1850. He came by way of Presidio, Texas, his exact birthplace or date is unknown to me. Upon Texas gaining its independence from Mexico and becoming a Republic, my great-grandfather became a Texan, and upon Texas joining the Union, he became an American citizen. According to my grandaunt's memoirs, my paternal great-grandmother was a Cherokee woman by the name of Maria De Los Angeles Samaniego. Although a Bracketville, Kinney County, Texas census shows her name, simply, as Maria Lara. She was born in Mexico in 1855. Since my grandaunt knew my great grandparents first-hand, I take hers information to be correct. Although, my grandfather's death certificate shows his mother as having been Maria Escobedo, this, attested to by the signature on the death certificate by a daughter of his, my aunt, Maria Lara Lomas. This causes me some emotional conflict, as I don't know which name to honor, although, I favor the Cherokee name because as I have stated, my grandaunt Eloisa knew my great-grandparents firsthand.

In my grandaunt's memoirs, she shares some very interesting and heart-warming stories concerning my great-grandfather, Blas. One of them is her recollection of the times he would take her to see her husband, my granduncle, Eugenio Lara, the trips being several miles from Del Rio and done by a horse-driven wagon. The purpose of these trips was to visit my granduncle, at which time my great-grandfather would bring his son some corn, watermelons and other foodstuff; something he also did for his other son, my grandfather, Hilario. Another heart-warming memoir my grand aunt penned down was of the times she used to go visit my grandparents and look after their first-born, my father. She states how much she enjoyed these visits and how much she enjoyed looking after my father.

A most endearing recollection of hers was of the time my great-grandfather was taking her back to Del Rio after one of such visit to my granduncle. Some distances from Del Rio, there were two water tanks known as the "Twin Tanks", these serving as a watering spot for travelers and their horses. During this particular time, there had been some heavy rains and the surrounding area around the tanks had been flooded, including the road that led to the tanks. My great-grandfather, being very familiar with this road, but not realizing how deep the water was, approached the watering area as usual. Before he knew it, the horse was belly-high in water! As the water was rising onto the wagon, my grandaunt placed her children on top of her belongings as far up on the wagon as she could. The wagon now being stuck, my great-grandfather stepped into the water, unhitched the horse, and one by one, took each of his grandchildren, on horseback, to high ground. My grandaunt, meanwhile, jumped into the water and swam out. She mentions that she was too embarrassed to have my great-grandfather pick her up and carrying her to higher ground. I find this portion of her memoirs warm, humorous and enriching. It is a close look into my great-grand father's life, his character and his devotion to his family. Reading her memoirs is like reading a Laura Ingalls Wilder, *Little House On the Prairie*, story.

There is another, colorful piece of literature my grandaunt penned down. It happened that on this one occasion, she was recovering from a fever for which the doctor had asked that her hair be cut off, in order to keep her body temperature down. After her recovery, for a period of time, family and friends called her "la pelona", or baldy; she was about eleven years old at the time. During this time, while playing on the front yard, my granduncle, Eugenio, came to visit her brother, Felix, who was a very close friend of his. My granduncle was riding a Pinto horse that was dressed up with a beautiful saddle and corresponding ensemble. Her brother was so impressed with this, that he asked my granduncle if he would sell it to him. My granduncle said no, but that he would trade the ensemble for "that little pelona," pointing to the young girl. Little did my granduncle know that the little "baldy" was to be his wife! On October fifteenth, 1901, they were married, she at the age of 15 years, eleven months and he, at the age of twenty-two years and four months; this is just as she wrote it. This is the extent of my genealogy on my father's side, with respect to his parents. My father had two brothers, Maclovio and Reynaldo and two sisters, Maria and Ester (Esther).

As to my paternal grandmother's side, Faustina Hernandez,

there is considerably more ancestral information, which, again, for which I am deeply indebted to my grandaunt, Eloisa. My great-grandparents on my paternal grandmother's side were Nazario Hernandez and Florencia Balboa. My great great-grandparents were Juan Pablo Hernandez (Cichimeca Indian) and Felipa Lomas Hernandez (Aztec/Mexican). My maternal great great-grandparents were Apolonio Galvan and Faustina Balboa (Spanish).

On my mother's side, my grandparents were Cayetano Payo Mendez, born in 1857 in Charcas, San Luis Potosi, Mexico and Marcelina Maldonado born in 1861 in the same town. From the Church of The Latter-Day Saints web site, I found that my paternal great-grandparents, on my mother's side, were Eduardo Mendez and Anastacia Payo Mendez. My great great grandparents were Juan Payo and Maria Regina Payo. My maternal great great-grandparents were Juan Maldonado and Sebera Mendoza.

My mother had two brothers, Jose and Isidrio and two sisters, Bernabe and Bonifacia. My mother's story is very interesting and heartwarming in itself. When my grandfather, Cayetano, passed away, my mother was only a little girl, probably six or seven years old. With encouragement and very little financial help from an uncle who lived in Rocksprings, Texas at the time, they embarked on a long journey from Charcas, Mexico, in the state of San Luis Potosi. They made it through Saltillo and into Monterrey, where they ran out of money and had to spend almost a year to earn enough money to continue their journey. In Monterrey, one of my uncles, Jose, (who was to be the grandfather of my "almost" girlfriend) worked in a pharmacy while the eldest, my other uncle Isidro, worked in a beer brewery.

Sometime after crossing into Texas, once again, they ran out of money and had to stay in a small down some distance from Rocksprings. This time, the whole family earned the money by picking cotton. A friend of the family from Rocksprings came by horse and buggy to take them home...the end of their journey. The family friend did not tell my grandmother, at the time, that her brother had passed away during their journey. Not long after arriving in Rocksprings, my grandmother passed away, both from the weariness of the journey, and the crushing news of her brother's death; she had gotten her children safely to Texas, to a better life; her journey had been completed.

MY GENEAOLOGY:
Father: Adolfo Hernandez Lara
Born in Del Rio Nov. 28, 1896
Died in San Jose, CA Jan. 24, 1980

Grandfather: Hilario Samaniego Lara
Born in Bracketville, Texas 1869
Died in Del Rio Sept. 21, 1938

Great-grandfather: Blas Lara
Born in Mexico 1850

Great-grandmother: Maria De Los Angeles Samaniego
Born in Mexico 1855

Lara uncles and aunts:
Reynaldo
Maclovio
Maria
Ester

Lara granduncles and grandaunts:
Dorotero born in 1868
Cayetana born in 1873
Simona Born in 1874
Octerena born in 1876
Eugenio born in 1879

Grandmother: Faustina Balboa Hernandez Lara
Born in Del Rio Sept. 11, 1889
Died in Bakersfield, California in 1951

Great-grandfather: Nazario Lomas Hernandez
Born in Mexico
Died in Del Rio in Nov. 1908
Great-grandmother: Florencia Balboa
Born in Eagle Pass, Texas
Died in Del Rio

Great great-grandfather: Juan Pablo Hernandez
Great great-grandmother: Felipa Lomas Hernandez
Great great-grandfather: Apolonio Balboa
Great great-grandmother Faustina Balboa

<u>Hernandez Grand uncles and aunts:</u>
Ramona
Faustina
Eloisa
Juan
David
Grabiel
Ester
Moises
Apolonio

Mother: Maria Julia Mendez Lara
Born in Charcas, San Luis Potosi, Mexico Feb. 28, 1900
Died in San Jose, California January. 1979

Grandfather: Cayetano Payo Mendez
Born in Charcas, San Luis Potosi, Mexico 1857
Died in Charcas, San Luis Potosi Mexico

Great-grandfather: Eduardo Mendez
Born in Mexico
Died in Mexico

Great-grandmother: Anastacia Payo
Born in Mexico
Died in Mexico

Grandmother: Marcelina Maldonado
Born in Charcas, S.L.P. Mexico
Died in Kerrville, Texas 1910

Great-grandfather: Juan Maldonado
Born in Mexico
Died in Mexico
Great-grandmother: Sebera Mendoza
Born in Mexico
Died in Mexico

Mendez uncles and aunts:
Isidro:
Born in 1882
Died in 1952 in Rocksprings, Texas

Bonifacia M. Flores:
Born in 1886 in Charcas San Luis Potosi, Mexico
Died in 1952 in Brady, Texas

Bernabe (aunt):
Born in 1890 in Charcas San Luis Potosi, Mexico
Died in 1919? in Rocksprings, Texas

Jose:
Born in 1894 in Charcas San Luis Potosi, Mexico
Died in 1978 in San Jose, California

My brothers and sisters:
Jose:
Born in Rocksprings, Texas in 1917

Died in Del Rio in 1952
Wife: Brijida Rincon
Children:
Jose Jr.
Roberto (Deceased)
Berta Patiño
Ruben (Deceased)

Bernabe:
Born in Del Rio in 1919
Died in San Jose, California, in1975
Wife: Paulina Rodriguez (Deceased)
Children:
Bernabe Jr.
Amparo (Deceased)
Dora
Johnny

Herminia:
Born in Del Rio in1921
Died in Del Rio in 2004
Husband (1st): Manuel Sanchez
Children: Elsa Jacobs
Husband: Pablo Salazar
Children:
David
Victor (Lenny)
Danny
Debbie
Denise

Epifania:
Born in Junction, Texas, in 1927
Died in San Jose, California in 2004
Husband: Santos Elemen

Children:
Maria Ester Piedad
Annabelia Flemate
Estella Dominguez
Richard
Sylvia Bullock
Santa Flores
Elizabeth Quiroz
Robert (Deceased)

Elida:
Born in Rocksprings, Texas, in1930
Husband: Anthony Thomas
Children: Patricia

Adolfo Jr.:
Born in Del Rio in 1932
Died in Modesto, California, in 2003

Mary Telles (1st wife)
Children:
Adolfo 3rd
Andrew

Anita Herrera (2nd wife)
Children:
Annette
Yvette
Pcarl
Linda
Sylvia

Eloisa:
Born in Del Rio in 1934
Died in Ceres, California, in 2002
Gabriel Ramos Jr. (1st Husband)

Children:
Julie
Terry
Angie
Gabriel 3rd (Deceased)

Max McMann (2nd Husband) (Deceased)
Children:
Alice

Ruben:
Born in Del Rio, Texas November 9, 1936
Gloria Estrada (1st wife)
Children:
Robert
Ruby

Judith Coleman (2nd wife)
Stepdaughters:
Lisa
Lori

Grandchildren:
Jessica Lara Moore
Jake Arioto Lara
Josh Arioto Lara

Step-grandchildren:
Alma Urbina Zazueta
Sara Murillio
Steve Listeri ((Deceased)
Jamie Listeri

Step great-grandchildren:
Marisa Zazueta
Alisa Zazueta

Minnie's family: Thanksgiving visit to Del Rio. Three sons, David, Lenny and Danny, two grandsons, Issac and Ray, live in California; two daughters, Dennise and Debbie, live in San Marcos, Texas.

Fane's family at Mendez family reunion July 16, 1995 at Cunningham Lake in San Jose. Annabelia, Estela, Maria Ester, Richard, sister Fane, Santa and Elizabeth.

Currie's family: daughter Patricia with husband, Robert, their son Fermin and daughter Regina holding granddaughter, Angelica.

Locha's family: Julie, (Danny, Minnie's son, Dora, Chato's daughter, Currie and me) Terry, Alice, Angies and Julie's daughter, Sarah

Dofo's family: wife Anita (far right), L. to R.) daughters Sylvia, Linda, Pearl, Yvette, and Annette. Dofo had two sons, Adolfo 3rd, and Andrew, with first wife Mary Telles.

The Dynamic Duo..anniversary dance.

A favorite photo of mine: My uncle Jose Mendez, mother's brother, my parents, and my aunt Maria Lomas, father's sister.

My parent's wedding anniversary

Left to right: sisters Eloisa (Locha), Elida (Currie),
Epifania (Fane) and Herminia (Minnie), father and mother,
brothers Bernabe (Chato), Adolfo Jr. (Dofo) and the kid from
Del Rio.

Brother Jose, who would have been next to mother, had
passed away a few years earlier.